W9-ATU-147

WHAT'S BREWING
in New England

WHAT'S BREWING
in New England

A Guide to Brewpubs
and Microbreweries

Kate Cone

**DOWN
EAST
BOOKS**

Copyright © 1997 Kathleen Ellen Cone
ISBN 0-89272-387-4

Cover photograph by Jim Dugan
Cover photograph location courtesy Sea Dog Brewing Company,
Camden, Maine
Design by Tim Seymour Designs, Camden, Maine
Printed and bound at Bookcrafters, Inc.

2   4   5   3   1

Down East Books
P.O. Box 679
Camden, Maine 04843

Library of Congress Cataloging-in-Publication Data

Cone, Kate, 1953-
    What's brewing in New England : a guide to brewpubs and
microbreweries / Kate Cone.
        p. cm.
    Includes index.
    ISBN 0-89272-387-4 (pbk.)
    1. Microbreweries—New England. 2. Bars (Drinking
establishments)—New England. I. Title.
TP573.U6C66 1997
647.9574—dc21

                                                            97-313
                                                            CIP

In memory of Jordan S. Cone,
1981–1997
Put in a good word for me up there.
I think I'm going to need it.

CONTENTS

ACKNOWLEDGMENTS

I owe many people much gratitude for their help in putting together this book. I first thank the brewpub and micro owners and brewers for answering questions and sending material, especially Richard Pfeffer and Ed Stebbins of Gritty McDuff's, Dan Feiner and Tony Vieira of brew moon, Will Meyers of Cambridge Brewing Company, and Mike LaCharite of Casco Bay Brewing Company. Thanks also to the various states' Departments of Tourism and the American Automobile Association (AAA) for the Area Attractions information.

For expressing confidence in my ability to write about beer, I thank Brett Peruzzi, of *Yankee Brew News*, Bev Walsmith of *Brew Magazine*, Jim Dorsch, formerly of *BeeR the Magazine*, Tom Dalldorf of *The Celebrator*, Peter Terhune of *Ale Street News*, Barbara Bartels of the *Bath-Brunswick Times Record*, and Al Diamon, of *Casco Bay Weekly*.

For allowing me to appear on the Maine Brewer's Web site, I thank Chris Haaland. For answering my Internet plea for opinions about the New England micro scene, I thank my Internet friends Simon Wesley, Rikk Desgres, Brian Cacciapouti, Russell Mast, Kit Wilcox, Ken Smith, Kevin Blanton, Chris van Hasselt, Jeff Fabijanic, Paula Phaneuf, and Roland Legault.

Thanks are due to Kit Anderson, who conducted beer tastings for my enlightenment and who also gave me home-brew lessons; Fred Forsley and Alan Pugsley of Shipyard Brewing Company for my first "taste" of the micro life; friends Jerry Healy and Rod Philbrick, mystery writers who thought a beer book was a nice way to get published; Jim "with the Jag" Moore for his support and the infamous ride to Stone Coast Brewing Company; the staff of Maine Writers and Publishers Alliance for much-needed empathy and encouragement. I also extend my gratitude to the staff at Down East Books, for pulling this book together and making it far more readable than it was originally.

Many thanks to Pat Theberge and Elaine Roccia of Cruise Vacations in Medford, Massachusetts, who were gracious hosts for my Boston research; my children, Sam, Burke, and Megan, who trekked through brewpubs and micro's with me. And special thanks to my husband, Bob Theberge, who understands how much it hurts not to write. Without his financial and technical support, this book wouldn't have seen the light of day.

—K.C.

FOREWORD

I'm reminded this St. Patrick's Day that it wasn't so long ago in New England that the nearest thing to exotic beer one could find was the green stuff served once a year to honor the Irish. Those were ugly times, in which defenders of good beer were forced to take refuge in the back room of Three Dollar Dewey's, with little more to sustain us than a few cases of Ballantine India Pale Ale, a couple of six packs of Narragansett Porter, and a lot of skunky-tasting imports. It's a wonder we survived. It's a wonder we remember.

But so far, the old memory seems to be working fine, because I'm also reminded of settling into a seat in a nondescript London pub in 1984 and realizing the place offered a half-dozen locally produced beers, three of them cask conditioned. If only it could be like this at home, I thought, that would be heaven.

Welcome to heaven. In this town, every neighborhood bar worth spitting on has installed at least a couple of taps devoted to the pioneering brews of David Geary, the proselytizing works of Alan Pugsley, or the adventurous spirits of Ed Stebbins and Richard Pfeffer. The better bars all have a range of beers that would put the best joints in London to shame, not to mention the top tap houses of Munich, Prague, or Brussels.

And it's not just this town. At Back Bay Brewing in Boston, I recently had a best bitter that was as good as anything John Bull ever dreamed of. The taste of the pilsner from Oak Pond Brewing Company in Skowhegan, Maine, summoned up a Prague spring. Ipswich's barley wine; Sugarloaf's IPA; pale ales from Flying Goose, Bray's, and Andrew's; stout from Belfast Bay (Maine, not Ireland); lagers from Greg Noonan's pubs and Belgian double ale from Allagash all flood my consciousness with one unmistakable message.

Which, unfortunately, I can't seem to remember.

But who cares. These day's, there's plenty of fresh, local beer wherever I go in the Northeast. 'Gansett Porter is history, Ballantine IPA is but a damp shadow of its former glory, and the imports still smell like Pepe Le Pew's boudoir. But the fine folks at Catamount, Boston Beer Works, and Atlantic Coast have mitigated my mourning for the bad old days in the trenches. The war is over, and the good guys have won.

Now it's your turn to sample the fruits of victory. Grab this book, a designated driver, and a few fistfuls of cash, and head out to experience the singular pleasures New England brewers have prepared. Checking out the local stuff is, after all, a lot cheaper than a tour of the world's most famous beer-making cities—and a lot easier on the memory—than hanging out in the old back room at Dewey's.

Cheers.

Al Diamon
March 17, 1997
Portland, Maine

(*When he remembers, Al Diamon writes the column "Politics and Other Mistakes" for* Casco Bay Weekly *in Portland.*)

INTRODUCTION

The ironic aspect of an introduction is that for you, the reader, it marks the beginning of a journey that for me has come to an end—at least for now. As I write this, I am finishing my eighteen months of research, starting you on the road to visiting the brewpubs and microbreweries in New England, and introducing you to the people who run them and to the visions and goals of these entrepreneurs. And like the New England weather, the brewpub and micro climate is volatile—if almost a hundred of them isn't enough, wait a minute. More are opening every day. *What's Brewing in New England* will point you in the right direction to find and taste the hand-crafted beers these brewers meticulously make and proudly serve or sell.

Who Am I?

Always the writer, I proposed this project to Down East Books after working as assistant to the president of Shipyard Brewing Company in Portland, Maine. The micro phenomenon was in full swing in Maine and elsewhere in New England, and a travel guide with a few food and home-brew recipes from the brewpubs and micro brewers seemed like an appropriate and much-needed volume.

I Know Who You Are

Generally an author doesn't get to know her readership until after the book is in print and feedback is given. But in my case, because of the presence and influence of the Internet, I feel that I already know you. Many of you responded to the requests for input I posted at Internet sites such as "Homebrewer's Digest," "Alcohol Temperance History Group," "Chileheads Digest," "Dorothyl (a mystery discussion group to which I post in reference to my other writing life: mystery fiction), and you visited my guest spot on the "Maine Brewer's Page." You helped put this travel guide together, E-mailing me your comments about various brewpubs and micros, describing their food and beers, making suggestions about the format of the book and how to make it most useful, and even taking photographs of the places to which I could not go because of the severity of last winter's weather. I know that you love good beer and that you will travel a fair distance to taste new brews and old favorites. I know that you value the quality of a brewpub's beer over its food, ambiance, or parking facilities. I know that you are traveling primarily to taste those beers and that other activities in the area of a pub or micro are ancillary at best and bothersome to think about at worst. I also know that most of you are men. In my traveling for this book and giving beer tastings, I've discovered that the people who stay in the room with the beer longest are the men. I have even been told by the wife of an avid home brewer, "I don't know how anyone can drink this stuff!" My observations lead me to speculate that women over fifty years old, who grew up when—in some parts of the country—it was considered "unladylike" to drink beer, are the ones hardest to convince of the new microbrews' positive attributes. But women forty-five and under, my age group, began college just in time to be "liberated" from such archaic views. We drank beer with the best of our male counterparts, and we continue to experiment with different brews, ask probing questions about beer styles and the brewing process, and learn to home-brew. And as word gets out that women began this whole thing thousands of years ago, more of us will enter the fold. Give it a couple of years.

In light of the current one-sidedness of the microbrew population's gender, though, I have figured a way to make *What's Brewing in New England* accessible, valuable, and fun to both beer lovers and their "non-beer-drinking significant others." Primarily for this group, I have included "Area Attractions" that list activities or events other than visiting brewpubs or going on micro tours. And, allowing one concession to political correctness and respect for my gender, I do not always recommend shopping as an alternate activity. After all, have you ever seen the baseball-hat and T-shirt tables at a beer festival? Shopping is not solely a female phenomenon!

Having said that, however, I would be remiss in excluding mention of such places as the Kittery, Maine, outlet area (a quick drive from the Portsmouth, New Hampshire, pubs) or the Freeport, Maine, outlets and L.L. Bean (a half-mile from the Freeport location of Gritty McDuff's Brewpub) or the huge gallerias of Boston (a subway ride or walk from several great pubs).

One Man's Meat . . .

I must stress that I am primarily a writer, not a beer expert. In *What's Brewing in New England,* I write about where to find microbrewed beers and do not pass judgment on them. Like most of you, I'm still learning about beer styles and what qualities make a style true-to-form or off-form. As a journalist, my first job is to give accurate information; I hope that I do so in an entertaining way. I prefer to defer to bona fide experts when necessary and to let the brewers speak for themselves about their creations.

Nor do I choose to rate the food found in the brewpubs. That would necessitate my visiting every one and trying many different dishes while there—an attractive but impossible task. I did visit many of the pubs and micros, and I will offer my impressions when appropriate. I will also pass on the comments of my Internet friends in regard to specific beers and dishes that were outstanding and made a place especially worth traveling to. I found from my E-mail feedback that you often disagreed with each other about the same brewpubs. Some of you loved the food at one establishment, others thought it was not so great. And the same was true for the beers. I hope that, as readers of this book, you will be adventurous and will experiment, deciding in the process whether you liked the places you visited and whether you would return.

No End in Sight

When will the microbrew phenomenon bottom out? Experts predict that the 1,000-plus micros existing now in North America will multiply to more than 4,000—the pre-Prohibition level of the last century. Michael Hall, owner of Global Brewing Services in Portland, Maine, has set up more than twenty-five micros stateside and worldwide, including one in Siberia. He agrees with that prediction, citing the rapid return on investment enjoyed by the owners of the breweries and brewpubs he has built. Such quick success means there is room for others, since the demographics of most cities indicate a need many brewers, restaurateurs, and entrepreneurs will be eager to fill. That's the bright side. For me, the down side is that it's nearly impossible to be completely up to date when micros are springing up seemingly overnight, like mushrooms after a good rain.

Nonetheless, I have made the best possible effort to be comprehensive when putting together *What's Brewing in New England.*

First, I used the following publications regularly, combing them for word of new micros: *Yankee Brew News, Ale Street News, Brew Magazine,* and *Celebrator Beer News.* As already noted, I constructed a web page and had it posted on the "Maine Brewer's Page" in a call for information and opinions about micros others had visited. I had my page listed on the major search engines available on Netscape. I posted messages on many individual web pages relating to beer, even E-mailing the micros that were on line and letting them know about my book.

I called state liquor-licensing offices, brewers' guilds, and state departments of tourism. I asked micro owners and brewers for word of other entrepreneurs. All were very sharing; if they knew of a new place, they told me. I called directory assistance endlessly to find the phone numbers of establishments for which I had only names. I completed as many as three mailings to all of the micros whose addresses I could procure. I made multiple follow-up phone calls to all of those micros that got my mailings.

Still, as we go to press, some of those brewers, owners, or marketing people have not responded to my calls or letters. So I have listed as much information about their pubs and micros as I could glean from other sources. Hopefully, *What's Brewing in New England* will become the standard micro travel guide for New England, and the holdouts will be eager to participate in future editions.

From the micros and brewpubs whose people did respond, I got varying degrees of cooperation, which will be obvious as you read *What's Brewing in New England.* Some were thrilled to participate, and the recipes, beer descriptions, photos, and fascinating background material they sent me reflects their interest in luring you to their brewpubs or micros to sip the beer and enjoy either the food or the tour. I hope you succumb.

Kate Cone

Harpswell, Maine

E-mail: katecone@ime.net

URL: http://w3.ime.net/~katecone

How to Use
What's Brewing in New England

I have included in each brewpub's or micro's entry the information it conveyed to me. Where the entry lacks information—such as hours, directions, or parking—such guidance was not provided. A good rule of thumb when traveling anywhere is, "When in doubt, call ahead," and that's especially true in New England, where most retail or service businesses operate on seasonal schedules that change often.

If you're headed for Boston and Cambridge, adjacent municipalities in Massachusetts, it is always advisable to park outside the city and take a subway or bus. The in-town parking garages are expensive, and you must battle traffic to get there. The Massachusetts Bay Transit Authority operates buses, subways, and above-ground trains to all areas where the pubs are located in both cities. Call MBTA at 617-222-5000 to request a printed schedule.

Directions can occupy a lot of space, especially when the traveler could be approaching from four different directions. Having listed almost 100 pubs and micros, I could have devoted the same number of pages just to directions. I have included them where they are short and simple. I suggest that you visit the web pages of the places that have them and print out directions for the pubs and micros you want to target. Or, call and have them mail directions to you; many have printed maps for this purpose. Or just take down their instructions over the phone.

Some brewpubs and microbreweries are located near enough to one another to make tours of several possible in a day or weekend. These "clusters" are listed at the beginning of the chapter, with a cross-reference to the page where each entity is described in detail.

A final note: One approach to visiting New England's brewpubs and micros is to go during the off-season. So, if you want to see ski-area facilities like the Shed in Stowe, Vermont, or Sunday River Brewing Company in Bethel, Maine, or Theo's at Sugarloaf, go during the spring, summer, or fall. By contrast, the coastal pubs will welcome you with open arms and full pint glasses (or mugs) if you visit during the winter, when they're slowest. The brewer will likely have more time to spend with your tour or even to give you an individual look around. In fact, if you visit during the dead of the off-season, you could get trapped in an existentialist heaven— a cross between *Waiting for Godot* and *No Exit:* They wait around for you, and when you arrive, they won't let you go.

MAINE

In Maine there are three areas where several microbreweries/brewpubs are in relatively close proximity. These groupings are given below, along with a consolidated list of area attractions that are also worth a visit.

PORTLAND AREA

Allagash Brewing Company (see page 5)
Casco Bay Brewing Company (see page 13)
D.L. Geary Brewing Company (see page 15)
Gritty McDuff's Brewpub (see page 18)
Shipyard Brewing Company (see page 27)
Stone Coast Brewing Company (see page 29)

AREA ATTRACTIONS

Portland, Maine is a super place: You can easily drive into the city and around in it. There's a lot of parking (though not necessarily on the street), and you'll discover a gorgeous, charming Old Port section with dozens of art galleries, unique clothing and jewelry stores, restaurants, and the dynamic duo of tap houses: Three Dollar Dewey's and—uptown—the Great Lost Bear. Other points of interest include:

- **The Children's Museum of Maine**
  142 Free Street; Portland, ME 04101; 207-828-1234
  Designed to entertain and educate kids up to age fourteen, the museum features a model space shuttle, a farm, bank, and grocery store, a seven-foot-diameter globe that floats and rotates on a jet of air, and many other hands-on exhibits.

- **Portland Museum of Art**
  7 Congress Square; Portland, ME 04101; 207-773-ARTS
  The museum's permanent collection focuses on state of Maine artists like Marsden Hartley, Andrew Wyeth, and Winslow Homer, so if you missed the Homer exhibit at Boston's Museum of Fine Arts, catch some of the paintings here. You can also drive to Prout's Neck (off Cape Elizabeth) and see Homer's studio and former home on one of

the most exclusive pieces of land on the Maine coast. The cliff walk around Prout's Neck is stunning, and if you're flush, you can stay over at the Black Point Inn, where Paul Newman used to vacation with Joanne.

• **Portland Head Light**
1000 Shore Road, Fort Williams State Park, Cape Elizabeth, ME 04107; 207-799-2661
One of the oldest lighthouses in continuous use, Portland Head Light was built in 1791, under the authorization of newly elected President George Washington. There are a museum, several walking paths, picnic facilities, and ocean everywhere.

• **Wadsworth-Longfellow House**
487 Congress Street; Portland, ME 04101; 207-879-0427
Shipyard Brewing Company's president and co-owner Fred Forsley is enamored of Henry Wadsworth Longfellow and asked his partner Alan Pugsley to create a beer honoring the Portland poet. Longfellow Winter Ale is the product of that devotion, and part of the proceeds of Shipyard's annual Longfellow birthday party goes toward the upkeep of this house. The first brick house built in Portland, this structure was commissioned by the poet's maternal grandfather and contains furniture, records, and personal possessions of the Wadsworth and Longfellow families.

The site of Longfellow's birthplace, at the corner of Fore and Hancock Streets, just happens to be where Shipyard maintains its Portland facility and is memorialized with a plaque. Photos of the original house, which was torn down in the 1950s, are a featured part of the Shipyard Brewing Company tour.

MIDCOAST AREA

Belfast: Belfast Bay Brewing Company (see page 9)
Camden: Sea Dog Brewing Company (see page 25)
Freeport: Gritty McDuff's Brewpub (see page 18)
Lincolnville: Andrew's Brewing Company (see page 6)

AREA ATTRACTIONS

Freeport, Maine, is *the* outlet capital of New England. It's the only place that contains the original L.L. Bean store, which—like Gritty's—is open 365 days a year. And, though Gritty's isn't open twenty-four hours a day, L.L. Bean is. So, you can stay at the classy Harraseeket Inn down the street, sneak out at 4 A.M. to do a little shopping, and stash the haul in the trunk of the car before your beer-loving companion stops reading the backs of his eyelids.

The Camden area offers gorgeous walking and driving along the coast. Skiing in winter and water sports in summer will keep you busy, and quaint shops in Camden village, just a few blocks from the Sea Dog, will entertain. See for sure:

- **Farnsworth Art Museum**
  19 Elm Street; Rockland, ME 04841; 207-596-6457
  The Farnsworth features artists with Maine connections—the Wyeths (N.C., Andrew, and Jamie), Fitz Hugh Lane, Winslow Homer, John Marin, and Louise Nevelson—as well as the work of other Americans and Europeans.

- **Owls Head Transportation Museum**
  State Route 73; Owls Head, ME 04854; 207-594-4418
  Get your fill of antique aircraft, autos, motorcycles, bicycles, and carriages, all in operating condition. Demonstrations are available in the summer.

Patrick Mullen, owner of Belfast Bay Brewing Company, recommends "one of the best marine museums in the country":

- **Penobscot Marine Museum**
  Church Street [just off U.S. Route 1]; Searsport, ME 04974; 207-548-2529

For more information, contact:

Belfast Chamber of Commerce: 207-338-5900
Rockland-Thomaston Area Chamber of Commerce: 207-596-0376.
Rockport-Camden-Lincolnville Area Chamber of Commerce: 207-236-4404
Searsport Chamber of Commerce: 207-548-6510

BAR HARBOR AREA

Atlantic Brewing Company/Lompoc Cafe (see page 6)
Bar Harbor Brewing Company (see page 7)
Jack Russell's Brewpub and Beer Garden (see page 22)
Maine Coast Brewing Company (see page 23)

AREA ATTRACTIONS

Bar Harbor is located on Mt. Desert (pronounced "dessert") Island, much of which is protected from development as Acadia National Park. The park is a 50-square-mile visual paradise, combining rugged Maine coastline with the majesty of more than fifteen mountains. Acadia is open year round, but a couple of the scenic roads are closed in winter. For hikers, there are 120 miles of trails and 44 miles of graded carriage roads for walking, biking, cross-country skiing, and jogging. Park naturalists offer programs for visitors between mid-June and Columbus Day.

Acadia is the most beautiful place I've ever visited, and the views of ocean meeting mountains are too breathtaking to pass up. For more information, contact Superintendent, Acadia National Park, P.O. Box 177, Bar Harbor, ME 04609, 207-288-3338.

Allagash Brewing Company

100 Industrial Way; Portland, ME 04103; 207-878-5385

Tours: By appointment
Gift shop: Yes

Rob Tod has never home-brewed a batch of beer in his life. He preferred to jump right into the microbrew fray by opening Allagash in July 1995 and offering his Belgian-style beers to Greater Portland aficionados. His decision to brew on a bigger scale, however, was not without much preparation. Tod, who hails from Carlisle, Massachusetts, graduated from Middlebury College with a degree in geology. After a few years of traveling, he returned to Vermont, where he went to work at Otter Creek Brewing Company.

"It was supposed to be a part-time job," Tod explains, "but the company was growing so quickly, my position grew from washing kegs to learning all aspects of the micro business—from cleaning tanks, brewing, and bottling to doing lab work. I did just about everything while I was there."

Why did Tod choose Portland, Maine, as a site for his brewery? And why Belgians? The twenty-seven-year-old has his reasons: "I saw Portland as an area for good growth potential. There is a keen awareness among local beer drinkers about microbrewed beers, a lot of interest, and more people to drink it than some other places in northern New England. And no one there was making Belgian-style beers. My choice to brew Belgians is based partly on love for the styles and partly on marketing," says Tod. "They are distinctive and unique, yet accessible and very drinkable—and, again, no one else was making them here."

What are his goals for the future? "Right now, I want to get Allagash beers into the major accounts in the Portland area, then expand outward from there." In summer 1996, Tod began bottling.

The Beer: Allagash White Beer and Allagash Double Ale are available on draught in Portland at the Great Lost Bear, Brian Boru, and Three Dollar Dewey's; in Brunswick, you'll find them at Joshua's and Benzoni's. Allagash Brewing Company is located in the same industrial complex as D.L. Geary and Casco Bay Brewing Company. You can hit the "Bermuda triangle" of micros on the same day!

Andrew's Brewing Company

RFD 1, Box 4975; Lincolnville, ME 04849; 207-763-3305

Tours: By appointment

Owner/brewer Andy Hazen is happy to report that his microbrewed beers are in such demand that distributors are begging him to bottle the stuff. Called "a national treasure" by Maine columnist and beer devotee Al Diamon, Andrew's beers are currently available on tap in Portland at Three Dollar Dewey's, the Great Lost Bear, and Bleachers. Elsewhere in the state, taste the brews at most of the major ski areas, in the Camden/Rockland area, and soon, due to the diligence of his distributors, throughout Maine. Hazen chuckles when he quotes Diamon's assessment of his Pale Ale: "hoppy enough to stun a rhino." With production climbing steadily at 100 percent a year, it won't be long before Hazen breaks down, buys or borrows a bottling line, and ships to the other New England states. After all, a "national treasure" begs to be appreciated on a regional scale.

Atlantic Brewing Company

30 Rodick Street; Bar Harbor, ME 04609; 207-288-9513

Tours: Daily at 4 P.M. (May to October)
Gift shop: Open daily from 10 A.M. to 6 P.M.

The Lompoc Cafe & Brewpub

34–36 Rodick Street; Bar Harbor, ME 04609; 207-288-9392

Hours: Daily from 11 A.M. to 1 A.M. (May to October)

Music: Nightly at 9 P.M.

The ales served in the Lompoc Cafe became so popular that Doug Maffucci had to open a brewery to make an adequate supply for customers who wanted to take these brews home. From a one-barrel system in 1990, Atlantic Brewing company has expanded to produce 50,000 gallons of brewer Roger Normand's five styles of ale per year. Content to market their beers only in Maine, Maffucci and Normand and crew serve up their eclectic menu, both food and beers, during the height of the tourist season, from May through October. Music is available nightly at 9 P.M.

The Beer: Atlantic Brewing Company describes its brews:

> **Bar Harbor Blueberry Ale**—One of Lompoc's most popular beers. Each batch of the English-style amber ale is made with the juice of more than 200 pounds of Maine wild blueberries, which results in a bluish-red color and an unmistakable blueberry aroma.
>
> **Ginger Wheat Ale**—A summer-style ale hopped with fresh ginger, yielding a crisp ginger aroma and dry finish.
>
> **Coal Porter**—An assertive porter offering generous hopping and malt body. This ale is cellared to create a mocha, smoky quality in the aroma.
>
> **Lompoc's Pale Ale**—A straightforward ale hopped with Perle, yielding a grassy aroma while keeping a sweet balance.
>
> **Bar Harbor Real Ale**—A smoothly sweet, nut-brown ale, lightly hopped.

The Food: Lompoc Cafe's menu focuses on Mediterranean cuisine and offers several vegetarian dishes, as well as the seafood that is the trademark of the gorgeous Bar Harbor area.

Bar Harbor Brewing Company

HC 30, Box 61; Route 3, Otter Creek Road; Bar Harbor, ME 04609; 207-288-4592

Tours: Call ahead for times.

Tod and Suzi Foster are celebrating the Beverage Tasting Institute's selection of their Cadillac Mountain Stout as the 1996 winner of the platinum award in its category, a big honor for these committed microbrewers. Tod welcomes visitors and says that they have a nice log cabin where you can sample their beers after the tour.

Bear Brewpub

36 Main Street; Orono, ME 04473; 207-866-2739

Tours: Available on request

Milos Blagojevic is brewer/ owner of this cozy pub, which is close to shopping and the University of Maine campus. As reported by my steady correspondent Simon Wesley, the atmosphere is "dark without being oppressive." There is a beer garden (complete with wall murals) at the front of the pub, and the place seats about fifty people in addition to those at the bar.

The Beer: The Bear's beers are unfiltered, and the list contains Crow Valley Blonde, Great Works Blonde, Berry Blonde Ale, I'll Be Darned Amber, Honey Bear Brown, Tough End Porter, and Midnight Stout.

The Food: The Bear has "great food," declares Andy Hazen, the owner/brewer of Andrew's Brewing Company in Lincolnville, Maine (see page 6). The menu leans heavily toward standard pub fare, and considering the Bear's college-town location, that's logical; few students have the income to be dining on haute cuisine. But there are standouts among the

Milos Blagojevic and a helper man the booth at the Third Annual Maine Brewers Festival.

standards: Bear-brew onion rings; ale-steamed mussels; pesto and arti-choke pizza; crab, spinach, and mushroom strudel; grilled lemon-pepper chicken, served in a sandwich or as an entrée; and baked vegetarian ziti. Otherwise, enjoy pub selections like "Wings of Fire," homemade soup (varies daily), potato nachos, sandwiches and burgers, a couple of salads, baby back ribs, chili, fish and chips, and a grilled Reuben sandwich.

Belfast Bay Brewing Company at The Ice Cream Barn Restaurant & Pub
100 Searsport Avenue; Belfast, ME 04915; 207-338-2662

Tours: Daily at 4:30 P.M. or by appointment.

The first thing Patrick Mullen will tell you about his venture into brewing is that he's the luckiest guy in the world to have brewer Dan McGovern, the former owner of Lake St. George Brewing Company. "He makes the best beer in Maine," declares Mullen proudly.

Head brewer Dan McGovern and owner Patrick Mullen at the Third Annual Maine Brewers Festival

McGovern explains why Lake St. George folded last fall. "My partner, Kellon Thames, and I were selling a lot of beer, but we needed to grow. In our case, growing meant finding $700,000 to fund an expansion." That proved to be an impossible sum for McGovern, a full-time meat cutter, and Thames, who works in a local graphic-design firm. So, in a classic "Catch-22" situation—making good beer but not being able to grow—Lake St. George became the first of the twenty-five Maine microbreweries and brewpubs to close.

But McGovern's loss was Mullen's gain. As soon as Patrick heard Dan was available, he asked him to head up the Belfast Bay brewing operation on a custom-made system designed by Doug Maffucci of Atlantic Brewing Company in Bar Harbor. Helping McGovern in the brewery is Chip Wick, who trained at the Wynkoop Brewery.

The Beer: Belfast Bay Oatmeal Stout was the beer McGovern and Mullen were pouring at the Maine Brewer's Festival in November 1996, but other brews will round out the list in 1997.

The Food: The Ice Cream Barn's kitchen is run by a chef who makes his own pastries and serves such mouthwatering Down East fare as lobster pie, prime rib, and a twenty-two-ounce T-bone steak. For the kids, or the kid in all of us, there's the homemade ice cream.

Berwick Brewing Company

105 Wild Rose Lane; South Berwick, ME 03903; 207-384-5847

Tours: Not available

Gift Shop: No

Neil Bryant is a chemical engineer whose love for home-brewing has grown into a cottage industry.

The Beer: Berwick Brown Ale is the flagship beer that Bryant is placing in Maine seacoast restaurants and bars. On a rotating basis, he will offer Berwick Stock Ale and, in winter, Berwick Maple Porter. Licensed in

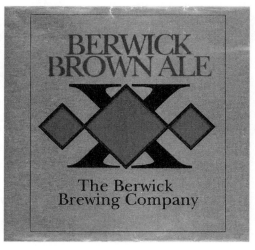

1995, Berwick Brewing Company was in full-scale production in spring 1996. Call the number listed above to find out where Bryant's beers can be tasted. One place that is already carrying them is the Cape Neddick Inn on Route 1 in Cape Neddick, Maine.

Bray's Brewpub and Eatery

Routes 302 and 35 (at the lights); P.O. Box 548; Naples, ME 04055; 207-693-6806

Tours: Summer tours, daily at 1 P.M. Off-season tours given on request if the brewer is available.

The story of how Bray's Brewpub came into being should be accompanied by the theme to *Twilight Zone.* The way Michele Windsor tells it, she and her husband, Michael Bray, went to college in Maine, spent the next thirteen years in the Pacific Northwest, then decided to open a brewpub back in Maine. Their choice of Naples was based on such marketing principles as traffic count,

KATE CONE

visibility, area demographics, and parking availability. The 150-year-old, mansard-roofed Victorian at the intersection of Route 302 and Route 35 fulfilled all those requirements. What Michele and Michael didn't know until they opened the Eatery in August 1995, was that two of the town's founding fathers shared their last names. Washington Bray and William Winsor helped settle the town of Naples more than a hundred years before, and both men lived within a quarter-mile of the present location of the pub. (Michele points out that her last name was spelled without the "d" until her great-grandfather added it eighty years ago.) Bray has been brewing at capacity since introducing his own beers in December 1995. "There is no fresher beer in the Lakes Region than this," he says. "There are no bottles, no kegs; it goes fresh from the brewery to your glass."

The Beer: Dispensed from his 3½-barrel, homemade system are Brandy Pond Blonde Ale, Old Church Pale Ale, and Pleasant Mountain Porter; the pub's fourth tap will be dedicated to a seasonal beer of Bray's choosing. Bray also serves many other microbrewed beers, and root beer will be brewed and served soon.

The Food: Heading up the culinary effort at Bray's is John Dugans, a native Mainer who has been a chef for fifteen years. Windsor describes Dugans as a "rare and wonderful find," maintaining that "without John, we'd just be another 'grub-pub.' " Among the menu selections served up by Dugan are: lobster stew with scallions and brandy; Maine crabcakes with smoked tomato coulis; a sausage platter with bratwurst, hot Italian, and whiskey-fennel sausage steamed in beer and served with

Owner/brewer Mike Bray (left) and his brother Rich, Assistant Brewer.

crusty bread; a pulled-pork sandwich, southern style, with Bray's barbecue sauce; twin petits filets of beef tenderloin, wrapped in bacon, pan roasted, and served au jus with Portobello mushrooms; shrimp in garlic butter with mushrooms and scallions on linguine; and fresh native scallops baked with honey and Dijon mustard.

Chef Dugans shared two recipes with us. I tried the mussels on New Year's Eve and loved the different twist andouille sausage gives this popular dish.

STEAMED MUSSELS IN BRAY'S ALE *(Makes two servings)*

> 3 cloves garlic
> 3 tablespoons olive oil
> Half an andouille sausage, sliced ¼ inch thick
> Half a roasted red pepper, diced
> ½ cup Bray's Ale
> 1 tablespoon butter
> 1½ pounds fresh mussels, debearded and cleaned

Combine the first six ingredients in a sauté pan. Heat until liquids boil. Add mussels. Cover, and steam until mussels open.

Baby Back Ribs in Bray's-Ale Barbecue Sauce

1 rack (approximately 2 pounds) baby back ribs
1 cup water
1 cup Bray's Ale
3½ cups Barbecue Sauce (see below)

Peel the back from the rack of ribs. Cut into three-rib sections and place on a rack in a pan, with the water and Bray's ale. Cover the pan, and put into a preheated, 350° oven for four to five hours, or until the meat pulls easily from the bone. Cool the ribs and cover them with the barbecue sauce.

Bray's Ale Barbecue Sauce

Combine 1 cup chili sauce, 2 cups ketchup, ¼ cup molasses, ¼ cup Bray's Ale, and one dash each of cayenne pepper, Worcestershire sauce, horseradish, and mustard. Add Liquid Smoke to taste.

Casco Bay Brewing Company

57 Industrial Way; Portland, ME 04103; 207-797-2020

Tours: Wednesday evenings at 6 P.M. and by appointment

Gift shop: Open Monday through Friday, from 8 A.M. to 5 P.M.

Internet access: Casco Bay Brewing Company is featured on "The Maine Brewer's Page" (Brew ME) at http://www.maine.com/brew/welcome.html.

Everything that you see at Casco Bay Brewing Company, makers of Katahdin beers, is a product of owner Mike LaCharite's beginnings as a basement home-brewer. "It's a hobby gone wild," he comments, showing off the impressive brewery, bottling line, and state-of-the-art kegging machine, nicknamed

KATE CONE

"Elvis." LaCharite, who won awards for his home-brews before he went pro, is a certified national beer judge and founder of the largest home-brew club in Maine, the Maine Ale and Lager Tasters (MALT). Since evolving from home-brewer to microbrewer, Casco Bay's president has graduated from the Siebel Institute in Chicago, one of the most prestigious brewing schools in the United States. Partner Bob Wade, a former Hannaford Brothers supermarket-chain executive, serves as Casco Bay Brewing comapny's executive vice president and treasurer.

Owner/brewer Mike LaCharite at the bottling line.

The Beer: LaCharite named his brews after the highest mountain in Maine:

Katahdin Golden—Cold lagered after a two-week fermentation, Golden has a clean, crisp flavor and light color and body that were designed to appeal to imported-beer drinkers. Hence its slogan, "The Import Alternative."

Katahdin Red Ale—Brewed in a hearty Irish style, Katahdin Red is full-bodied with a complex malt flavor. "Step ahead and have a Red."

Katahdin Stout—Flaked oats give this smooth stout a creamy texture, and Belgian specialty malts balance any bitterness derived from roasted barley, allowing this stout to claim it has "A Mountain of Flavor."

Also: Pale Ale and Seasonal Spiced Brew.

D.L. Geary Brewing Company

38 Evergreen Drive; Portland, ME 04103; 207-878-BEER

Tours: Monday through Friday; call ahead for an appointment.

Gift shop: Open Monday through Friday, 8 A.M. to 4 P.M. Items are also available by mail.

If one person is responsible for igniting the microbrewery fire under the East Coast, it's David Geary. In 1986, he was the first to open a non-contract micro east of the Mississippi, making him the "granddaddy" of New England microbrewing. Enjoy the D.L. Geary tour, buy some brewmania, and talk brewing with Geary and his crew, which includes his daughter, Kelly Geary Lucas. After that, head out to the Great Lost Bear (right down Forest Avenue) to enjoy sampling all three of the industrial park's brews: Allagash, Casco Bay, and D.L. Geary's.

Owner/brewer Dave Geary.

The Beer:

Geary's Pale Ale—A classic British pale ale in the tradition of the beers of Burton-on-Trent. Copper colored, dry, clean, and crisp with lots of late hop flavor.

Geary's London Porter—Faithfully recreated English porter, with deep mahogany color and restrained malt flavor.

Geary's Hampshire Special Ale—Geary's contribution to the seasonal market, featuring a huge toasted-malt flavor balanced by assertive hoppiness. This ale is listed as one of the top twenty-four North American beers described on Michael Jackson's Beer Hunter CD-ROM, which is based on the program produced last year for the Discovery Channel.

Also: Geary's American Ale.

Federal Jack's Restaurant and Brewpub

Western Avenue; Kennebunk, ME 04043; 207-967-4322

Tours: Call for times

Gift shop: The Maine Traders Giftshop is located in the same retail complex and carries all Shipyard giftware and beers.

Located in the slim area of the Kennebunks known as "Taint Town" (because, accord-ing to local lore, "'Taint Kennebunk and 'taint Kennebunkport"), Federal Jack's brewpub was the first place to serve Shipyard beers. It was called Kennebunkport Brewing Company then and had its humble beginnings as a seven-barrel Peter Austin brewing system. Helping Fred Forsley and brewmaster Alan Pugsley install the equipment were Ed Stebbins and Richard Pfeffer of Gritty McDuff's Brewpub. Since its opening in 1992, "KBC," as it was fondly called, expanded to include Shipyard Brewing Company's huge brewery in Portland, then was returned to the Forsley/Pugsley fold after Miller Brewing Company bought into Shipyard. Through the metamorphosis, however confusing, KBC has retained its seven-barrel charm and waits for you to tour. Then head upstairs to Federal Jack's.

The Beer: All of Shipyard's brews are served on tap or in bottles. The big event of the year is in December and is called Prelude Weekend, when all of Kennebunkport comes

out to open the Christmas season. Santa even arrives in port aboard a lobster boat. Commemorated in Prelude Ale, this is a perfect off-season time to visit the coast of Maine and hole up at Federal Jack's after the tree-lighting ceremony.

The Food: Appetizers include " 'Taint Town Shrimp," steamed in 'Taint Town Pale Ale; mussels steamed in Goat Island Light Ale, with fresh basil and garlic; Walker Point Atlantic oysters, breaded and fried; and steamers with drawn butter. Entrées also feature fresh Maine seafood but cater to the crowd that wants grazing and pub fare.

Area Attractions: The Kennebunks have exclusive shops, galleries, and old homes to explore. Beautiful beaches beckon all year long; of special note to parents is one called "Mother's Beach" because of its adjacent playground. Traffic here gets heavy in the summer, but it's much improved all around because George Bush, whose family has summered at Walker's Point for years, is no longer our president.

For complete information packets call the Kennebunk/Kennebunkport Chamber of Commerce at 207-967-0857 and the Kennebunkport Information and Hospitality Center at 207-967-8600.

Great Falls Brewing Company

36 Court Street; Auburn, ME 04210; 207-784-3919

Tours: On request

Brewer Cass Bartlett has an amazing background, and if you have a couple of hours, he will tell you about it. Cass grew up in Massachusetts but points out that his entire family now lives in Maine. He was a mental-health professional for many years, specializing in geriatrics, and before that he was a professional actor, starring in stage productions that ran from light comedy to Shakespeare. Still

Brewer Cass Bartlett.

involved to some extent in community theater, Bartlett now spends most of his time brewing at Great Falls.

The Beer: Some of his specialties include Auburn Amber, Bobcat Brown, Mad Dog Porter, Court Street Wheat, Raspberry Wheat, and Bartlett's Pale Ale. On the list of seasonals are Irregardless Ale and Holiday Wheat. Downstairs at The Cellar Door, Great Falls offers live music, emphasizing blues and R&B.

Great Falls beer can be sampled at The Cellar Door.

Area Attractions: Auburn grew up as a manufacturing center, as did many of the river cities in Maine and elsewhere in New England. At the height of its success, factories sent as many as two million pairs of shoes per year to other parts of the world. Auburn is about an hour away from skiing at Sugarloaf and Sunday River, and it hosts Lost Valley Ski Area, a small facility perfect for kids. Since it's right off I-95, Auburn is a perfect stop on the way to Bangor or places north. For other activities, call the Androscoggin County Chamber of Commerce at 207-783-2249.

Gritty McDuff's Brewpub

396 Fore Street; Portland, ME 04101; 207-772-2739

Tours: Saturday and Sunday at 1 P.M. or by request

Gift shop: The "Brewtique," as Gritty's calls it, is open Thursday through Monday, 10:30 A.M. to 6 P.M.; Sunday, from noon to 6 P.M.

The crash of '87 pretty much put Gritty McDuff's owner Richard Pfeffer out of a job as a stockbroker. What else to do but open a brewpub in the heart of Portland's charming Old Port? Co-owner and brewmaster Ed Stebbins was also ready for a career change. Selling books had its appeal, but after some time living in England, Stebbins was ready to offer his own beer instead.

"Maine's Original Brew-pub" is Gritty's slogan, since it was the first such eatery/drinkery in Maine and the first U.S. brewpub set up by Shipyard's Alan Pugsley. In their radio commercials, Richard and Ed bill themselves as "just a couple of guys really into beer," and Gritty's is a friendly place, where "the guys" are almost always on hand and willing to have a

KATE CONE

beer with you. The oversized windows that grace this 1870 brick building overlook the harbor, and large pub tables line the dining room, inviting customers to mingle and talk over traditional pub fare.

Voted "Best of Portland" just about every year since its opening in 1988, Gritty's has a mug club with a two-year waiting list. For fifty dollars a year, members receive discounted prices on their pints and a good-looking mug waiting on a hook above the bar for their arrival. Patrick Chisholm of Portland is a five-year veteran of the mug club and recites his membership number (#102) proudly, declaring, "Gritty's is a place for everyone!"

The Beer: Ed Stebbins brews McDuff's Best Bitter, Portland Head Light Pale Ale, Black Fly Stout, Lion's Pride Brown Ale, and Sebago Light Ale. Seasonals include Christmas Ale, Winter Wheat, Oatmeal Stout, Long Winter Ale, Old Porter, Abbey Style Ale, India Pale Ale, and Pumpkin Ale.

Among their many honors, Richard and Ed were asked to brew a special beer to celebrate the inauguration of Maine's governor, Angus King.

Teaming up with David Geary, the trio came up with "Inaugurale, Fit for A. King." The name was nothing short of brilliant, and the beer was brilliantly received at the ball, to which everyone in the state of Maine was invited.

From the Internet come these recommendations: For beers, Roger Stillman likes Black Fly Stout, Nuptial Ale, and Portland Head Light Ale. For food, he goes for the knockwurst and blue-cheese burger.

Owner Richard Pfeffer at the Portland Brewers Festival.

Gritty McDuff's Brewpub (Freeport)

Box 328; Lower Main Street; Freeport, ME 04032; 207-865-4321

Internet access: www.grittys.com

E-mail: grittys2ix.net com.com

Tours: Saturdays at 3 P.M. or by request

Gift shop: The "Brewtique" at the front of the pub is open seven days a week, from noon to 7 P.M., but merchandise is available during all business hours. Just ask a staff person, and someone will open it for you.

The Freeport Gritty's has been packing them in ever since its July 1995 opening. Located about a half-mile from L.L. Bean, Gritty's features a slightly different menu than the Old Port location, emphasizing traditional pub fare, grazing food, stone-oven pizzas, pasta, seafood, chili, burgers, sandwiches, and salads.

Gritty's diners can look down on the Freeport brewery from this large window.

I can attest to the satisfaction level of the club sandwiches. My eleven-year-old son, Burke, wanted to order two sandwiches. "One isn't going to fill me up, Mom," he argued. After laboring over a single, enormous turkey-and-bacon club, which was served with thick, wavy potato chips, he almost had to be carried

Gritty's Brewtique.

out to the car. If one sandwich can fill that kid's stomach, it's a bargain at any price.

Even heartier pub selections are all created by Gritty's and include knockwurst steamed in Best Bitter Ale and served with beans; Cornish pastie; steak-and-kidney pie; chicken and sweet-potato pie; and shepherd's pie cooked with Black Fly Stout. Two specialties that are uniquely Gritty's are "Roasted Garlic Soup" and "Black Fly Stew." The recipes follow.

GRITTY McDUFF'S BLACK FLY STEW

1 tablespoon vegetable oil
1 pound bottom round stew beef
4 large onions, chopped
2 pounds peeled potatoes, chopped
   into 1-inch cubes
2 bay leaves
4 pints Gritty's Black Fly Stout
1 pint beef stock or water
Salt and pepper to taste

Brown lightly floured beef in vegetable oil. Add onions, and sauté until lightly browned. Add beer, water, and seasoning. Cook until beef is almost tender. Add potatoes and cook until they are tender. Thicken with a roux made from ½ cup melted butter and flour.

Gritty's Roasted Garlic Soup

4 onions, sliced
8 bulbs roasted garlic
¼ cup fresh garlic, chopped
1 pint Gritty's Best Bitter
6 cups chicken, vegetable, or beef stock
1 teaspoon thyme
1 teaspoon black pepper
1 tablespoon salt
2 bay leaves
3 potatoes, peeled and cubed

Sauté onions in vegetable oil until soft. Add fresh garlic and sauté for 1 minute. Add stock, beer, bay leaves, and potatoes; bring to a boil. Reduce to a simmer, and cover for about fifteen minutes. Add roasted garlic, salt, pepper, and thyme. With a potato masher or hand mixer, mash garlic and potatoes until soup is fairly thick. Serve in bowls, with garlic-bread croutons and chopped parsley.

Jack Russell's Brewpub and Beer Garden

102 Eden Street; Bar Harbor, ME 04609; 207-288-4914

Tom St. Germaine's second brewpub venture debuts with a large outdoor beer garden. You can play croquet and other lawn games while you sample eight draft beers, two cask-conditioned ales, or homemade root beer. Last year Tom and his crew made twenty-two different beers. This year they'll try to top that. The menu will include British pub food, a one-pound pork chop, lobster, locally smoked salmon, clam chowder, and personal-size pizzas.

Kennebec River Brewery at Northern Outdoors

Route 201; P.O. Box 100; The Forks, ME 04985; 207-663-4466;
800-765-7238

Internet access: www.northernoutdoors.com
Tours: Yes; call for details.

Jim Yearwood has brought his own microbrewed beer to this outdoor-adventure resort, where he has worked for seventeen years. Located thirty miles south of Jackman, Northern Outdoors will take you (in season) rafting, rock climbing, hunting, or snowmobiling and can accommodate up to 400 guests in campsites or cabins. You have to visit to sample Jim's brews, which are not available elsewhere. A home-brewer for seven years, Jim makes Penobscot Porter, Magic Ale IPA, and Northern Light (a blond style) on a four-barrel Pierre Rajotte system. The brewpub features homemade American cuisine.

Maine Coast Brewing Company and the Taproom

P.O. Box 826; 21A Cottage Street; Bar Harbor, ME 04609; 207-288-4914

Internet access: http://www.acadia.net/mcbrew

E-mail: tomst@barharbor.acadia.net

Tours: Daily; call for times.

Gift shop: Located in pub. Open daily from 11 A.M. to 1 A.M.

Tom St. Germaine wants to make perfectly clear the reasons he launched his brewing company: (1) He wanted to make beer purchases tax deductible; (2) he saw it as his destiny to make great beer; and (3) he didn't want to have a real job, *ever!*

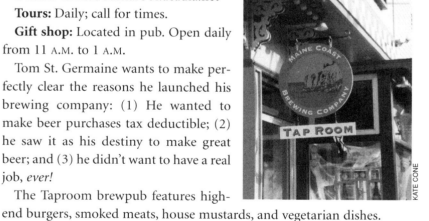

KATE CONE

The Taproom brewpub features high-end burgers, smoked meats, house mustards, and vegetarian dishes.

The Beer: Tom's brews are: Bar Harbor Gold (his flagship beer), Great Head Pale Ale, Redneck Ale, Eden Porter, and Sweet Waters Stout. Among his seasonals are Honey Wheat, IPA, ESB, Hefe Weisen, Imperial Stout, Dark Wheat, Double Bock, and an extra strong Golden Ale. Maine Coast participates in the Boston Brewer's Festival, so if you can't make it as far as Bar Harbor, you can visit Tom and crew there. If you get to Portland, try Tom's beers at the Great Lost Bear.

Narrow Gauge Brewing Company and the Granary Brewpub and Coffeehouse

Box 609; 23 Pleasant Street; Farmington, ME 04938; 207-779-0710

Narrow Gauge has been producing beers for The Granary since January 1996. Located at the gateway to the Rangeley Lakes

Head brewer Karl Wegner draws a pint while Joe Levigne looks on.

and the Sugarloaf and Saddleback ski areas, this pub is a great place to stop on your way north.

The Beer: Available only on the premises, the selection includes Clearwater Cream Ale, Sidetrack Amber, Boxcar Brown, and Coal Porter.

Oak Pond Brewing Company

Oak Pond Road; Box 1208; Skowhegan, ME 04976; 207-474-5952

Oak Pond owner Pat Lawton's accomplishments and quests have made her a sort of Renaissance woman. She is an artist and photographer, and — turned on to microbrewed beer by a taste of Geary's — she has added "microbrewery owner" to that list.

The **Beer:** Oak Pond's beer selections include Northern Light Pale Ale, which at press time was available at Bloomfield's in Skowhegan, as well as Somerset Lager and Nut Brown Ale, which are available at many additional pubs and restaurants across the state.

The Oak Pond Brewing Company crew await the crowd at the 1996 Maine Brewers Festival.

Sea Dog Brewing Company

43 Mechanic Street; Camden, ME 04843; 207-236-6863; and 26 Front Street; Bangor, ME 04401; 207-947-8720; 888-4-SEA DOG

Hours and tours: Call for times.

The Sea Dog's two locations serve the coast and the center of Maine with an extensive pub and seafood menu, along with brewer Dennis Hansen's well-regarded beers. Internet correspondent Dan Fitzgerald claims the Camden Sea Dog was his favorite Maine brewpub on a recent vacation spent sampling several such establishments.

The Sea Dog Brewing company occupies a beautiful complex in the town of Camden.

The **Beer:** Flagship beers are Black Irish Winter Stout, Penobscot Maine Pilsener, Windjammer Blonde Ale, Owl's Head Light, Old Baggywrinkle ESB, Old East India Pale

Ale, and Old Gollywobbler Brown Ale. Seasonals include wheat, blueberry, pumpkin, Oktoberfest, and Doppelbock. Specials are made three to five times a month; past selections have been Toasty Nut Porter, Maine Tartan Scottish Ale, Celtic Red Ale, Cat's Whiskers Cream Ale,

and Nor'easter Barley Wine. Sea Dog recently added a hazelnut porter to their bottled beer lineup.

The Food: A dinner menu was not provided, but lunch at the Sea Dog features Maine seafood (fresh and smoked) and plenty of pub selections like soups, chili, salads, and sandwiches. There are many non-alcoholic drinks, as well as good wine-by-the-glass and single malt scotches.

The Sea Dog in Camden has a mug club, and for extra-loyal regular customers there's an added perk: you can have your name carved into your favorite barstool. So far, only "Louie" and "Cal" have earned the treat.

Tables at the Sea Dog overlook the Megunticook River.

Sheepscot Valley Brewing Company

RR 1, Box 88, Townhouse Road; Whitefield, ME 04353; 207-549-5530

Tours: By appointment

Owner/brewer Steve Gorrill has been in business only since 1995, but there is already a steady demand for his product.

The Beer: Among Sheepscot's offerings are Madgoose Belgian Ale; White Rabbit, a Belgian white he offers in summer; and Highlander Scottish Ale, brewed in fall and winter. Steve will be glad to give you a tour, but if you can't make it inland to Whitefield, try his brews at Three Dollar Dewey's or the Great Lost Bear in Portland. Steve occasionally guest-bartends at some of the Portland tap houses. Call ahead to find out when his next gig is; he'll serve you his beers and tell you all about them.

Shipyard Brewing Company

86 Newbury Street; Portland, ME 04101; 207-761-0807

One-stop shopping at The Shipyard.

Internet access: http://www.shipyard.com

Tours: Daily from 3 P.M. to 5 P.M.

Gift shop: Summer hours are 10 A.M. to 9 P.M.; for off-season hours, call ahead. This is the biggest micro store in New England. It carries Shipyard's own line of brew-clothes called "Shipwear," the entire line of beers, games, beer books, stuffed animals, and more. Call 1-800-BREW-ALE for a product catalog or to place an order.

In 1992, real estate consultant Fred Forsley was hired to come up with some ideas for an ailing retail complex in Kennebunk. His first thought was to convince the owners of Gritty McDuff's Brewpub to open a second site there. They declined, but suggested that Fred himself open a brewpub with the help of Alan Pugsley, a consultant for Peter Austin and Partners, a British company that specialized in setting up microbreweries and

brewpubs. Pugsley had gotten David
Geary started as well as Gritty's, and
after some discussion, agreed to
work with Forsley to create some
winning brews for Federal Jack's
Brewpub and Kennebunkport Brewing Company (see page 16).

So "winning" were Pugsley's brews,
that the business outgrew the seven-
barrel system in Kennebunk. Within
two years, Forsley brought Pugsley
on as a full partner and brewmaster
and was looking up and down the
midcoast area for a second brewery
location. Enticed to Portland by tax

*Head brewer Paul Hendry chats
with visitors at Brewers Fest.*

incentives bestowed by the city, Forsley decided on a four-acre site on the
waterfront, which before urban renewal's wrecking ball, had been the
birthsite of the poet Henry Wadsworth Longfellow. After much renova-
tion, Forsleys and Pugsley's new company, Shipyard Brewing Company
(SBC), started operations in 1994.

In 1995 Forsley and Pugsley entered into an agreement with American
Specialty and Craft Beer Company, a subsidiary of Miller Brewing Company. The union gave the SBC owners the capital needed to complete a
third expansion and increased distribution strength and marketing exper-
tise, yet allowed them to retain their authority. Forsley continues in his role
as president and Pugsley enjoys full control over the brewery. By late 1996,
SBC was producing 89,000 barrels of its beers, then numbering ten.

Available in New England, the Mid-Atlantic states, Georgia, and
Florida, SBC also has the distinction of being the first microbrewery to
locate in an airport. In October 1996, Shipyard announced that the
Greater Orlando Aviation Authority Board approved its plans to build
and operate a twenty-barrel microbrewery at the Orlando International
Airport.

The Beer: Shipyard Export Ale, Old Thumper Extra Special Ale, Blue Fin Stout, Goat Island Light, Shipyard Brown Ale, Chamberlain Pale Ale, Mystic Seaport Pale Ale. Seasonals include: Longfellow Winter Ale, Prelude Holiday Ale, and Sirius Summer Wheat Ale.

Stone Coast Brewing Company

14–26 York Street; Portland, ME 04101; 207-773-BEER

Opened in January 1996, Stone Coast is the effort of Sunday River Brewing Company's Grant Wilson and brewer Peter Leavitt (see page 30). Offering Cajun cuisine and emphasizing live music, Stone Coast offers a cigar bar which occupies the third floor of this energetically renovated and decorated historic building at the edge of the Old Port. Live music, billiard tables, and a bar share this cigar-lover's dream space.

Owner Grant Wilson draws a pint from hand-carved tap handles.

The Beer: Cannery Kolsch, named for the first commercial cannery in the United States at 12 York Street; 420 IPA, named for the 420th batch of this IPA brewed at Stone Coast's sister pub, Sunday River; Stone Coast Sessions; J.B. Brown Ale; 5 Points ESB; and Stone Coast Stout.

The Food: The menu leans

The best table in the house overlooks the brewery.

heavily to Cajun flavors, with a few Maine seafood items. Casco crab cakes, Kolsch-cooked shrimp cocktail, baked oysters, and a raw bar jump out to be ordered as appetizers. Sandwiches include shrimp, chicken, and oyster "po-boys," just like those in the bayous; a shaved-steak "bomb"; fish and chips; and a muffaletta. The list of entrées features sirloin steak, broiled haddock, grilled salmon, a variety of étouffées, and jambalaya.

Sunday River Brewing Company

P.O. Box 847; U.S. Route 2 and Sunday River Road; Bethel, ME 04217

Tours: Tuesdays at 2 P.M. and by appointment

Gift shop: The Beer Store (on the premises) offers items by mail order, as well.

Located at the base of the Sunday River Ski-way access road between Mt. Will and the Androscoggin River, SRBC opened in December 1992. Grant Wilson and Hans Trupp knew that locating a brewpub with entertainment at one of New England's most popular ski areas would be a winner. Time has proved their theory.

The Beer: The Moose's Tale Brewpub serves thirsty skiers freshly made beers. Mary Beth Brandt, the first woman head brewer in New England, offers Pyrite Golden Ale; Mollyocket IPA; her flagship beer, Sunday River Alt; Redstone Red Ale; Black Bear Porter; and seasonals made at her discretion. Sunday River Alt is also available in bottles throughout Maine.

The Food: Heavy on stick-to-the-ribs grazing food, the Moose's Tale menu features reasonable prices. The barbecue pit "spits" up baby back ribs, spare ribs, pork chops, pulled pork, chicken (breasts or a roasted half), or combinations of some of the above.

Tom Nostovick, Assistant Brewer, and Mary Beth Brandt, Head Brewer.

Area Attractions: The name of the game here is skiing.

• **Sunday River Ski Area**
  Information: 207-824-3000; Reservations: 1-800-543-2SKI

In summer, the Bethel area offers many opportunities for hiking, canoeing, and camping at Grafton Notch State Park. The Rangeley Lakes are close by, and Sunday River Ski Area has developed a mountain-bike park that has become quite popular. For more information, call the Bethel Area Chamber of Commerce at 207-824-2282.

If you don't ski but you do enjoy historical pursuits, check out the Bethel Historical Society, located in the Dr. Moses Mason House. Ask about Mollyocket. If you're not into history *or* skiing, try some shopping at these places: Bonnema Potters at Lower Main Street (207-824-2821); Books-n-Things at 162 Main Street (207-824-0275); S. Timberlake Co. on Church Street (a designer of wooden furnishings in the Shaker tradition; call 207-824-2234); and The Toy Shop at 162 Main Street (207-824-TOYS). Nearby is Perham's of West Paris on Route 26 in West Paris. Here you'll find custom jewelry featuring Maine-mined gemstones like aquamarine, tourmaline, and amethyst. The museum contains one of the finest collections of Maine minerals in the state.

Theo's Restaurant and Pub at Sugarloaf Brewing Company

RR 1, Box 2268; Access Road; Carrabassett Valley, ME 04947-9758; 207-237-2211

Tours: Call for schedule

The main reason you'd travel up this way is probably to ski Sugarloaf/USA, New England's biggest ski mountain, with a 2,820-foot vertical drop, 107 trails, the largest snowboard/alpine park in Maine, the largest half-pipe in the country, great grooming and forty-three miles of ski trails. But aprés your snowy self-abuse, find your way to Theo's,

where happy hour still starts every day at 4 P.M., and Chef MacMiller serves up pizza, burgers, salads, finger foods, and full dinners. Enjoy the new game room, with its seven-foot billiard tables, jukebox, bowling and video games, and live music on Wednesday, Thursday, and Saturday. Last year, Theo's featured a Sunday-night comedy spot with stars from HBO and Comedy Central. Carrabassett beers and ales are now available in bottles elsewhere in Maine.

Sugarloaf/USA

1-800-THE-LOAF

Internet access: http://www.sugarloaf.com/

E-mail: info@sugarloaf.com

Area Attractions: If you drive all the way up to Sugarloaf with your beer- and ski-loving partner, but you don't like beer or skiing, you'd better think about separate vacations, breaking up, flying to Reno or becoming a workaholic. Really.

NEW HAMPSHIRE

In New Hampshire there are two areas where several microbreweries/brewpubs are in relatively close proximity. These groupings are given below, along with a consolidated list of area attractions that are also worth a visit.

PORTSMOUTH AREA

Smuttynose Brewing Company (see page 41)
The Portsmouth Brewery (see page 38)

AREA ATTRACTIONS

Call the Seacoast Council on Tourism at 603-436-7678 or 800-221-5623 for more information. Some points of interest include:

• **Water Country**
  Route 1; Portsmouth, NH 03801; 603-436-3556
  New England's largest water park.
• **Strawbery Banke**
  603-443-1100
  Historic downtown section of Portsmouth dating from 1695 featuring tours, events, and exhibitions.
• **Kittery Outlet Malls**
  Route 1; Kittery, ME

WHITE MOUNTAINS

Laconia: Stone Coast on Winnipesaukee (see page 43)
Littleton: Italian Oasis Restaurant/Brewpub (see page 36)
Moultonborough: Castle Springs Brewing Company (see page 34)
North Woodstock: The Woodstock Inn (see page 43)

AREA ATTRACTIONS

The White Mountains offer much in the way of hiking, sightseeing, and skiing. Call the White Mountains Attractions office at 603-745-8720 or 800-FIND MTS for more information.

Castle Springs Brewing Company

Castle in the Clouds Complex; P.O. Box 131, Route 171;
Moultonborough, NH 03254; 603-476-8844; Fax: 603-476-5794

Tours: On weekends; there's a video tour in the lobby for "off" times.

Take a mountainside castle on 5,400 acres overlooking Lake Winnipesaukee, add crystal-clear spring water bottled right on the grounds, install a brewing system and brewer Richard Young, and the result is magic. After only four years in the bottled-water business, the very well-trained and savvy owners of Castle Springs water company have decided to use their pure spring water to make microbrewed beer.

Located at "Castle in the Clouds," a mansion built by millionaire Thomas Plant at the turn of the century, Castle Springs was started in 1992 by former R. J. Reynolds CEO J. Paul Sticht. The beer will be called "Lucknow," after the mansion, the history of which has been captured on videos that are nothing short of fascinating. At press time, an enthusiastic Mark Wiggins, executive vice-president of operations, assured me that the first three batches of Lucknow beer were in the fermenters. By the time you read this, all will be full-steam ahead.

The Beer: The brewing operations are headed by Richard Young, who will use a twenty-barrel DME system to produce Castle Springs' beers, which include Lucknow Munich-Style Lager, IPA, Porter, and an American Wheat. Although there is no brewpub in place at Castle Springs, there are restaurants nearby, and vis-

itors can partake of other activities like horseback riding, hiking, and a tram ride to the location of the spring that is the source of the company's water. Castle Springs will soon make a root beer to appeal to kids. The place is a perfect destination for beer lovers and their families.

Elm City Brewing Company

222 West Street, Unit 46; The Colony Mill; Keene, NH 03431; 603-355-3335

Elm City opened in December 1995 in what was a huge woolen mill that once made materials for Civil War troops. Owner Debbie Rivest told me that she and her colleagues smoke their own salmon and that their Texas-style chili took third place in the North Conway, New Hampshire, Chilifest last year. That makes a promising, mouth-watering start to their menu, which stresses sandwiches, soups, salads, appetizers, and pub dishes. Some

standouts are the salmon, brined in ale, then smoked and served on a board with fresh breads and Elm City mustards; an ale-marinated, grilled chicken-breast sandwich; and beer-battered onion rings.

The Beer: Brewer Tony Poanessa trained at the Siebel Institute in Chicago and professes to maintain the spirit of experimentation when concocting his beers. His West India Pale Ale is a classic IPA, but it is hopped with Cascade hops from the Pacific Northwest. On the traditional side, Tony's Pothole Porter is brewed to style, using English two-row malted barley and fresh, whole-flower English hops. Other Elm City beers include Lunch Pale Ale, Holy Grail Ale, Mill Creek Wheat, Oatmeal Stout (seasonal), and a brew listed only as Wing Nut.

Area Attractions: Restored in 1983, the Colony Mill now houses Elm City, as well as dozens of other specialty shops and antique dealers. Chances are you could browse the several buildings that make up the mill complex to the point that your beer lover would have to track *you* down. Emphasizing New England-made products, the mill establishments promise unique shopping, with in-mall entertainment like live music, strolling puppeteers, and seasonal events.

Flying Goose Brewpub at Four Corners Bar and Grille

Route 11; New London, NH 03257; 603-526-2327

The Beer: Head brewer Scott Brown has turned to local history for beer names. Heading up the list with Weetamo Raspberry Wheat and Weetamo Wheat, Brown puns from the Weetamo steamship, which used to deposit its passengers along the shores of Lake Sunapee for their summer vacations. Other brews include Split Rock Cream Ale, Pearly Town IPA, and a homemade root beer for the kids.

The Food: The menu sounds all-American, with sandwiches like barbecued beef and Philly steak-and-cheese, and main dishes like London broil, fish, and chicken.

Italian Oasis Restaurant/Brewpub

127 Main Street; Littleton, NH 03561; 603-444-6995

The Beer: John Mordello is co-owner and head brewer here. He bravely works his two-barrel system to produce Oasis Pale Ale, Cannon Amber, and Black Bear Stout. Bee Sting Wheat was created for the summer crowd, using fifteen pounds of honey per batch. The food menu is full-scale Italian.

Martha's Exchange Restaurant and Brewing Company
185 Main Street; Nashua, NH 03060; 603-883-8781

Internet access: http://www.marthas.com

Internet correspondent Peter Hayden and his crew thought Martha's was worth the fifty minutes it took them to get there, giving special praise to the Cajun scallops and veal Marsala. Martha's offers more than a dozen beers and its own root beer, which Peter says is "very good—better than the old drugstore root beer I had when I was a kid."

The Beer: Try Downtown Brown, Ale Capone IPA, Volstead '33 Lager, Bull Frog Stout, Untouchable Scotch Ale, Hefe Weizen, Honey Porter, White Mountain Wheat, and several others.

Area Attractions:

• **American Stage Festival**
   603-673-7515
   New Hampshire's largest professional theater presents Broadway musicals, comedies, dramas, and children's productions.

New Hampshire Custom Brewers
150 Franklin Street; Manchester, NH 03101; 603-624-0695; 888-777-0608

E-mail address: loonale.com

Tours: Call ahead.

Jon Thomas is using experience gleaned from stints at the Bitter End Bistro and Hill Country Brewery in Austin, Texas, to produce this new micro's Loon Pale Ale. Owners Tom Dufresne and Art Lyford opened in September 1996 and may have added other brews to their lineup by the time you read this.

Old Nutfield Brewing Company
22 Manchester Road, Rt. 28; Derry, NH 03038; 603-434-WORT (9678)

Tours: Friday at 5:30 P.M. and Saturday at 1 P.M. and 3 P.M.

Gift shop: Open Monday through Saturday from 12 noon to 5 P.M.

Internet access: http://www.nutfield.com

Owner/brewer Jim Killeen explains the history behind Old Nutfield: "In

April of 1719, a small group of families left
the port city of Derry, Ireland, and settled
just a 'barrel's roll' from our microbrewery
in what was then known as the Nutfield
Colony. In tribute to their pioneering spirit,
we have dedicated ourselves to the art of
brewing the freshest, full-bodied ales. Nutfield Ales are 'fire-brewed' in a brick brew
kettle and fermented in open vats just as they

used to do in the Old Country. This traditional brewing process takes a
little longer, but we're sure you'll agree it's worth it!" In operation since
August 1995, Old Nutfield is already firmly established in more than
1,000 retail stores and 200 restaurants.

The Beer: Working with a twenty-five-barrel brewing system set up by
Shipyard's Alan Pugsley, Jim Killeen turns out 650 cases from each batch.
He shipped his first brews to Massachusetts within three months of open-
ing his doors. Old Man Ale and Auburn Red Ale are also available in Maine.
After your tour of the brewery, visit the taproom, sample Old Nutfield's
brews, and buy six-packs and half-gallon "Nutters" to take home.

Area Attractions: Derry, New Hampshire, was the boyhood home of
Alan Shephard, Jr., the first American in space. Another famous resident,
from 1900 to 1911, was the poet Robert Frost. Visit his farm on State Route
28, where you can see period furnishings and a poetry display in the barn,
complete with video taped readings of Frost's poetry. Call 603-432-3091
from mid-June to Labor Day, or 603-271-3254 in the off-season.

The Portsmouth Brewery

56 Market Street; Portsmouth, NH 03801; 603-431-1115

Tours: By appointment (special parties of as many as 100 people can be
accommodated).

I received no response from the Eglestons when I inquired about their
Portsmouth facility, but a brochure picked up at the Boston Brewers Festival lists their offerings.

The Beer: Amber Lager, Blonde Ale, Black Cat Stout, Old Brown Dog (1989 Silver medal winner at the Great American Beer Festival), Golden Lager and Pale Ale.

The Seven Barrel Brewery

Rt. 12-A; West Lebanon, NH 03784; 603-298-5566

Tours: Arranged upon request.

Gift shop: Retail merchandise is on sale at the bar.

Home-brew Supply Store: Seven Barrel is the only brewpub in New England with its own home-brewer's supply store, open Thursdays and Fridays from 4 P.M. to 7 P.M. and Saturdays and Sundays at irregular times (call ahead).

The Seven Barrel Brewery is Greg Noonan's second location, opened in April 1994. West Lebanon is right over the Vermont line, near Dartmouth College, and is close to three other brewpubs and micros: Catamount, Jasper Murdoch Alehouse at the Norwich Inn, and Long Trail Brewing Company, formerly Mountain Brewers. And handily enough, Noonan located Seven Barrel halfway between Brattleboro, Vermont, home of Windham Brewery at the Latchis Hotel, and McNeill's Brewery, and Burlington, where his Vermont Pub and Brewery beckons thirsty travelers. If you're traveling for a long weekend, this brewpub trail is a fruitful one.

Noonan notes that the Seven Barrel Brewery is named for its "brew length": the system produces batches of seven 31-gallon barrels per brew. The post-and-beam brew house tower at the front of the building allows the curious to observe the brewing process from inside or outside the pub. Brewmaster Noonan is proud of his effort here, claiming to have the most traditional brew house in New England, from its gravity brewhouse design to its 1896 copper decoction kettle and a mash tun equipped with a rakes-and-paddle mixer.

The Beer: Seven Barrel offers more than a dozen regular beers at any given time, plus seasonals when the mood strikes or the season dawns. Among the regulars are IceRock Canadian Light, New Dublin Brown Ale, Old No. 7 Pale Ale, Champion Reserve India Ale, R.I.P. Imperial

Stout, Beetlejuice Wheat (Betelgeuse Weiss), Blueberry Cream Ale, Old H.P. Belgian Ale, Rocktoberfest, Draft Ox Dark Lager, Spuyten Duyvil Belgian Red, Wit's End Wit, and Buglight Light. By the time you read this, Noonan and White should have completed the installation of beer engines to accommodate three hand-pulled, cask-conditioned, dry-hopped ales. The drink menu features more than a dozen single-malt Scotches.

The Food: The pub seats 120 people and features a large, butternut-paneled non-smoking area that adjoins the sixty-foot, oak-paneled bar. The menu features a diverse range of pub specialties, including Cornish pasties, cock-a-leekie pie, mulligan stew, bangers and mash, toad-in-the-hole, bubble and squeak, shepherd's pie, Welsh rarebit, mulligatawny, and steak-and-onion pie. Quite unusual are the buffalo chili and the Vermont-raised venison and beefalo (cross-bred buffalo and beef cow).

Entertainment is available Tuesdays, Fridays, and Saturdays from 9:30 P.M. to 12:30 A.M., spotlighting local talent with a focus on the blues. Darts are popular on weekdays and weekday evenings.

Summing up the experience is Internet friend Paula Phaneuf, a Rhode Island college student who has quested through many New

Bartender Tim Howe.

England brewpubs: "My favorite . . . is Seven Barrel . . . it has a very cozy British-pub type of atmosphere, which can be attributed largely to their food. They serve typical British pub fare, but the food is anything but typical. All meals are reasonably priced, and more than reasonably delicious."

Area Attractions: This is flea-market heaven. Every Sunday, from May to October, one of the largest flea markets in the East takes place in the parking lot right outside the pub's doors. Noonan also notes that Seven Barrel is located in the heart of white-water canoeing country and sits within a half-hour's drive of a dozen ski resorts, including Killington and Mt. Sunapee.

Smuttynose Brewing Company

225 Heritage Avenue; Portsmouth, NH 03801; 603-436-4026

This is another Janet and Peter Egleston micro. Call for tour times.

Stark Mill Brewery and Restaurant

500 Commercial Street; Manchester, NH 03101; 603-622-0000

Tours: Upon request

Internet access: http://www.starkmill.com

Head brewer J. B. Smith claims it was just his love for beer that drew him to his current position working with fellow brewer Dan Pariseau and owner Peter Telge, an eighteen-year veteran of the restaurant business.

The Beer: Located at the center of the historic mill district in Manchester, Stark Mill Brewery keeps on tap Tasha's Red Tail Ale, about which Internet friend Peter Hayden had compliments; Mt. Uncanoonuc Light Cream Ale; General Stark Dark Porter; Amoskeag Golden; Milly's Oatmeal Stout; and a specialty brew featured each month.

KATE CONE

The Food: The menu at Stark Mill is casual, with the emphasis on inexpensive appetizers, pizzas, sandwiches, basic pastas, salads, and Middle Eastern dishes. Some menu items that jump out at you as being particularly appealing are homemade chicken-noodle soup (it's described as "just like Dave's Mom's"; I'm guessing Dave is the chef), blooming onion with Cajun ranch dressing, grilled eggplant and feta pizza, pub salad made with tricolor pasta, lamb-in-a-pocket, and broccoli, salami, and diced tomatoes in balsamic vinaigrette.

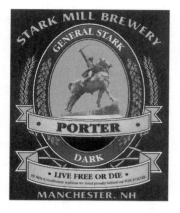

Otherwise, the food looks substantial and reasonably priced. Appetizers focus on the grazing variety: Louisiana grilled shrimp, chili, potato skins, Cajun fries, and buffalo wings among others. Entrees feature grilled items such as baby back ribs, T-bone steak, chicken breast, and catch-of-the-day. A vegetarian stir-fry is also avail-

able. Pasta dishes are traditional: Alfredo, carbonara, Bolognese, marinara, and fresh-tomato and basil with rotini, angel hair, linguini, fettucini, or penne.

Gyros, beer-steamed hot dogs, French dip, a Reuben, and grilled chicken head up the list of sandwiches, while international selections like kibbe, tabouli, hummus, and shepherd's pie round out this fill-your-tummy menu. Prices range from $3.95 to $11.95, and there are a few lower-priced items like a cup of soup or a soft pretzel.

The pub is located in a restored mill with spectacular brick-and-wood architectural features. An eighty-foot long bar overlooks the fourteen barrel DME brewing system, so patrons can watch the whole process. Seven televisions with three satellite feeds provide sports fans with ample coverage of any and all events. Pool tables and dartboards are located in the bar area.

Area Attractions:

• **Currier Gallery of Art**

194 Orange Street; Manchester, NH 03101; 603-669-6144

Call ahead to make sure the planned renovations were finished on schedule. This museum is located in a 1929 Beaux Arts building reminiscent of an Italian Renaissance palace. Exhibits include Western European paintings and sculpture from the thirteenth to the twentieth centuries; American paintings; glass, silver, and pewter; a large collection of New Hampshire-made furniture; and changing films, lectures, and concerts given year-round.

• **Palace Theatre**

80 Hanover Street; Manchester, NH 03101

Known for its excellent acoustics and larger-than-average stage, this 1915 theater has been fully restored and serves as home to the New Hampshire Performing Arts Center, the New Hampshire Symphony Orchestra, and the Opera League of New Hampshire. For more details and schedules of performances, call the Greater Manchester Chamber of Commerce at 603-666-6600.

Stone Coast on Winnipesaukee

546 Main Street; Laconia, NH 03246; 603-528-4188

Brought to you by Grant Wilson of Stone Coast Brewing Company in Portland, Maine, (see page 29) Stone Coast on "Winnie" features brewer Peter Leavitt's beers brewed in a fifteen-barrel system. The menu is similar to that in the Portland, Maine, location, as are the beers,

The Woodstock Inn

135 Main Street; North Woodstock, NH 03262; 603-745-3951; 800-321-3985

Who needs a tour when you can spend the weekend at the Woodstock Inn and brew all day Saturday with other guest/beer enthusiasts? For $125.00 per person (double occupancy), you'll stay in a quaint room in

Eileen and Scott Rice's century-old Victorian inn and be treated to a growler of their beer in your room upon your arrival; a Friday-night reception where you meet and mingle with your brew-mates; breakfast, then a Saturday brewing day where you will receive hands-on brewing experience; and lunch, followed by an eight-course dinner designed to pair one of Woodstock's beers with each course. You'll also walk away with a Woodstock T-shirt or baseball hat. For $175.00, you can have a room with a Jacuzzi.

The Beer: Lost River Light, Red Rack Ale, Loon Golden Ale, Pigs Ear Brown Ale, and Old Man Oatmeal Stout.

VERMONT

In Vermont there are two areas where several microbreweries/brewpubs are in relatively close proximity. These groupings are given below, along with a consolidated list of area attractions that are also worth a visit.

BRATTLEBORO AREA

McNeill's Brewery (see page 57)
Windham Brewery at the Latchis Grille (see page 64)

AREA ATTRACTIONS:

•**Brattleboro Museum and Art Center**
Main and Mount Vernon Streets; Brattleboro, VT 05301; 802-257-0124
Located in the former Union Railroad Station, four galleries present changing exhibits focusing on traditional and contemporary visual arts, as well as historical topics. More information about the area is available by calling the Brattleboro Area Chamber of Commerce at 802-254-4565.

Contact these sources for all the details.

• **Vermont Chamber of Commerce**
802-223-3443; Fax: 802-229-4581
E-mail: VT Chamber @InternetMCI.com
Internet access: http://www.genghis.com/vermont/discover.htm

• **Vermont Ski Area Association**
Internet access: http://www.genghis.com/skivermont/nebest/skivt.htm

• **Vermont Skiing Today Snowline Report**
800-VERMONT or 802-229-0531

BURLINGTON AREA

Magic Hat Brewing Company (see page 57)
Ruben James Restaurant and Brewery (see page 59)
Three Needs Taproom and Brewery (see page 62)
Vermont Pub and Brewery (see page 62)

AREA ATTRACTIONS

Burlington is the largest city in Vermont and offers many opportunities to appreciate the less-rural part of the state. Call the Lake Champlain Regional Chamber of Commerce at 802-863-3489 for scads of information on lake cruises and other seasonal events and activities.

- **The Discovery Museum and Planetarium**
  Route 2A; Essex Junction, VT 05452; 802-878-8687
  This hands-on children's museum and science center is open daily.
- **Vermont Teddy Bear Company**
  Route 7; Shelburne, VT 05482; 802-985-1322
  Tours are available at this sure-to-be-fun factory.
- **Church Street Marketplace**
  A four-block-long pedestrian mall in Burlington's historic district, the market hosts regularly scheduled events. Call 802-863-1648 for more information.

Bennington Brewers Ltd.

190 North Street (U.S. Route 7); Bennington, VT 05201; 802-447-3510

E-mail address: bennbrew@sover.net
Internet access: http://www.bennbrew~/sover.net
Tours: Call for details.
Hours: January through mid-May: closed Tuesdays and Wednesdays; otherwise, open from noon to 6 P.M. Mid-May through December: open Fridays from noon to 8 P.M.; otherwise, from noon to 6 P.M.

In the short year since they started Bennington Brewers Ltd., owners Frank Murray and Ken Ubertini have built an ambitious assortment of beers. Brewed on a sixty-barrel DME system and distributed throughout southern Vermont and upstate New York are Vermont Country Bridges, Peach Flavored Amber, Towhead Ale, Back Roads Ale, Raspberry Stout, Full Fashioned Apple Ale, and Strawberry Blond. At press time, brewer Frank Murray was contemplating a citrus-based beer and a Belgian wit beer for the coming summer season.

Black River Brewing Company
Black River Brew House

207 Main Street; Ludlow, VT 05149; 802-228-3100

Tours: Upon request.

Gift shop: T-shirts available for sale from 11 A.M. to 1 A.M.

Entertainment: Nightly live music

Owner/brewer Tom Coleman has built on his knowledge of the micro scene in the Pacific Northwest, where he and his wife, Teri, lived. Tom attended the University of California at Davis and the Siebel Institute to learn the brewing art and decided to take his experience to rural Vermont. Tom brews five standards and occasional specialty beers with his "homemade" one-barrel brewing system. Located near Okemo Ski Mountain, Black River is a logical stop on your way north from Brattleboro. An hour north of McNeill's and Latchis, and an hour south of the Seven Barrel Brewery, it's in the middle of your northward "climb" through Vermont.

The Beer: Big Buck American Premium Ale; Blind Faith, a standard pale ale; Ramblin' Amber Ale; Oh Be Joyful, a classic brown ale; and Brewer's Passion Porter.

The Food: Open for only a year at this writing, the Brew House has already won the Ludlow Chamber of Commerce "Judges' Choice" award for its black bean chili, and Tom says he also sells a lot of homemade

"Potato Porter Cheddar Soup." Prices don't climb above $8.95 and begin at $3.95 for the soups and chili. Other appetizers: toasted, fresh cheese ravioli with marinara sauce; beer-battered chicken fingers; beer-battered mushrooms; "Irish" nachos (potato skins with bacon, cheese, and sour cream); and black bean-covered nachos with salsa and sour cream.

Entrées lead off with bangers and mash, featuring native Vermont sausage; beer-battered fish and chips; and shepherd's pie. A generous list of sandwiches includes vegetable grill, with eggplant, zucchini, yellow squash; Portobello mushroom, onions, roasted red peppers, and minted chevre; turkey club with bacon, avocado, tomatoes, lettuce, and sun-dried cranberry with roasted-garlic-and-basil mayo; chicken breast that is first marinated in a tamari/Porter/ginger mixture, then grilled, topped with Swiss cheese, avocado, tomatoes, red onions, and lettuce, and served on crusty French bread; tempeh burger with Swiss cheese, roasted red peppers, red onion, sprouts and tamari/ginger mayo; and a hamburger with fixings on an English muffin.

POTATO PORTER CHEDDAR SOUP

¼ cup olive oil
2 onions
1 bulb garlic
2 pieces celery
1 carrot
15 russet potatoes
Herbs (bay leaf, thyme, coriander, white pepper, black pepper)
1 cup chicken stock
1 quart Brewer's Passion Porter
2 pounds sharp cheddar cheese
1 pint heavy cream
Kosher salt

Chop onions, celery, garlic, carrot, and potatoes; sauté in olive oil until translucent/soft. Add liquids, spices, and cheese; simmer 30 minutes, or until potato is soft. Pour in cream just before serving. Add salt to taste.

Ludlow's Award-Winning Black Bean Chili

10 pounds ground beef
2 onions
2 pounds black beans, cooked
1½ #10 cans tomatoes
½ teaspoon sage
1 tablespoon dry mustard
1 cup chili powder
1 cup curry powder
1 teaspoon thyme
½ teaspoon red pepper
Sugar

Brown the ground beef, then drain off excess fat. Chop onions and simmer in the ground beef until onion is translucent. Add black beans, tomatoes, and remaining ingredients. Simmer for three hours. Adjust spice to taste. Sugar should be used sparingly to counter the tartness of the tomatoes. A pinch or two should do it.

Area Attractions: All of Vermont is foliage heaven in the fall. As Tom Coleman points out, Okemo Mountain offers skiing. For more complete information, call the Ludlow Area Chamber of Commerce at 802-223-5830.

Catamount Brewing Company
58 South Main Street; White River Junction, VT 05001; 802-296-2248

Tours: July through October—Monday through Saturday at 11 A.M., 1 P.M., and 3 P.M.; and Sunday at 1 P.M. and 3 P.M. November through June—Saturday at 11 A.M., 1 P.M., and 3 P.M.

Gift shop: Open Monday through Saturday from 9 A.M. to 5 P.M., and Sunday from 1 P.M. to 5 P.M.

If you are at all tempted to drive by White River Junction and pass up the Catamount Brewery, *don't!* I concur with my Internet friends that

Catamount has the micro tour down brilliantly. Paula Phaneuf says: "As for micros, my favorite—by all means—is the Catamount Brewery. Not only do they make absolutely superb beers, their tours are among the most informative I have been on. They take you through the brewing process in detail, along with giving a history of the brewery, followed by a tasting of their beers. It is extremely helpful

Jeff Close describes the beers at a brewery tour.

for novice home-brewers, because the staff is knowledgeable and willing to answer any questions."

And Roland Legault describes Catamount as ". . . worth a visit, since it's one of the better breweries in Vermont, and they give a nice brewery tour."

The company's Jeff Close greeted us warmly, even though we were too early for the scheduled tour. He took me through the brewery anyway, then, when the rest of the crowd arrived, we went through the formal tour. Afterward we had a detailed, friendly tasting of all the Catamount brews.

The Beer: In a recent conversation with Close, who handles publicity and public relations for Catamount, he revealed proudly that their beer had been served at every Christmas reception hosted by the White House. The company's 1995 special Pale Ale proved so popular, it is being bottled and shipped to

The bottling line at Catamount.

Massachusetts and other states. Close mentioned that Catamount is always brewing at capacity, even with a recent addition of new tanks, and is contemplating opening another facility within a few years to handle the volume. Other beers are Catamount Gold, the Gold medal winner at the Great American Beer Festival; Catamount Amber; Catamount Porter; and Ethan Allen Ale.

Franklin County Brewery
The Brew Lab Hombrewer's Supply Store
94 North Main Street; St. Albans, VT 05478; 802-524-2772

Tours: On demand

The Beer: Owner Bennett Dawson produces Rail City Ale, which is available in Burlington and north of Burlington in more than forty restaurants. You can also buy it at some seventy-five stores, in half-gallon growlers and six packs.

Gallagher's Bar and Grill
Routes 17 and 100; Waitsfield, VT 05673; 802-496-8800

Tours: Call ahead.

Rob Parrish brews Mad River Stout and Sugarbush Ale for patrons of the Grill's pub fare.

Golden Dome Brewing Company
5 Pioneer Street; Montpelier, VT 05602; 802-223-3290

Gift shop: Beers and brewmania are available in the tasting room.

Tours: On demand

The Beer: Owners Ian Dowling and Russ Fitzpatrick offer Ceres Back Forty Amber Ale and Session Ale, as well as a lager, and a summer seasonal. These brews are available in Montpelier, Burlington, and in between. In Montpelier, try them at McGillicuddy's Irish Pub and Sarducci's. In Burlington, head to Manhattan Pizza and the Metronome. In Waterbury, belly up at Arvad's Restaurant.

Jasper Murdock's Alehouse and The Norwich Inn

325 Main Street; Norwich, VT 05055; 802-649-1143

The NORWICH INN

ESTABLISHED 1797

SIMON WESLEY

Let's jump right in with Internet correspondent Roland Legault's assessment of Jasper Murdock's Alehouse: "It's at the back of the Norwich Inn, which is stunning in itself. The beers are all good; the food is excellent. This is such a beautiful area that I have to recommend it highly." Roland declares that living for four years in Montreal, Canada, gave him ample opportunity to spend weekends in Vermont; hence his intimate knowledge of the area.

The inn itself is an awesome sight, inside and out. Owner Sally Wilson, whose husband, Tim, is the co-owner/brewer, has done an incredible job redecorating the gracefully aging building. When we visited, the Victorian parlor contained a huge Christmas tree, gleaming with period decorations. Tim put a 78-rpm Glenn Miller Orchestra record on his antique gramophone, then happily showed us around, even though we arrived unannounced.

The inn's guest book dates back to the millennium, or at least several decades, and is replete with not only names and addresses, but also cleverly sketched cartoons of the guests—mostly Dartmouth "men" cavorting over to Norwich for the weekend.

KATE CONE

There are also little messages and thanks to the then-owners for the great food and lodging (and quantities of drink, I suspect).

The Beer: Tim Wilson isn't afraid to wax creative in his small brew house, located in a renovated carriage house behind the inn. His beer list contains more than ten styles of brews, which are available only at the inn and in the alehouse. Among the beers you can try are Whistling Pig Red Ale, a garnet-colored, Irish-style red ale; Jasper Murdock's ESB, named for Colonel Jasper Murdock, who founded the inn in 1797; Elijah Burton's Mild Ale, a malty amber ale that features Golding hops and was named for one of Norwich's first settlers; Old Slipperskin India Pale Ale; Stackpole Porter; Short 'n Stout; Fuggle and Barleycorn; O.B. Joyful; Bronx Cheer the Raspberry Beer; and Heifer Vice Wheat Beer. Just listening to the stories behind the names of the brews will keep you entertained

all evening long. When I spoke with Tim a year after our visit, he was ready to bottle Whistling Pig, Stackpole Porter, Second Wind Oatmeal Stout, and Old Slipperyskin in twenty-two-ounce bottles for sale in the small retail shop at the inn.

The Food: The menu at Jasper Murdock's Alehouse is much less expensive than the dining room's, but the food comes from the same source. Chef Terrence Webb, who was trained at the Culinary Institute of America, leads this ambitious kitchen effort.

In the evenings, an investment of $2.95 to $7.95 will buy you: Caesar salad; soup of the day; creamed New England oysters; marinated, homemade mozzarella plate; grilled shrimp with Asian pasta salad; freshly baked quiche-of-the-day; southern-fried-chicken burger, fresh Maine crab cakes with lime/jalapeno mayo; chilled, pepper-crusted filet mignon sandwich; Jamaican jerk chicken wings; minted lamb with new-potato salad; baked, five-cheese angel hair pasta with spiced tomato sauce; and strudel filled with wild mushrooms, pine nuts, and chevre; shepherd's pie with a baby-red-potato crust; steamed Prince Edward Island mussels; cheese tortellini with prosciutto, mushrooms, and asiago cream; and house-smoked molasses duck plate.

In the dining room, lunch has a similar touch, repeating most of the pub selections and adding a few more sophisticated items. Dinner is higher end, reflecting the effort expended in the kitchen. Prices range from $13.95 for a vegetable strudel, to $19.95 for a grilled filet mignon with roasted-shallot Cabernet butter. Sundays treat guests and customers to a champagne brunch, where eggs Benedict, poached salmon fillet, Belgian waffles, quiche, omelettes, and crepes will help you forget that the weekend is coming to an end. Menus change seasonally.

Area Attractions:

• Montshire Museum of Science
   Montshire Road; Norwich, VT 05055; 802-649-2200
   Set on 100 acres along the Connecticut River, the museum offers exhibits on science, natural history, and technology; freshwater and saltwater aquariums; live animals and mounted specimens from around the world; and lectures, workshops, and hands-on exhibits.

Jigger Hill Brewery

Mailing address: P.O. Box 837 South Royalton, VT 05068
Street address: Dickerman Hill; North Tunbridge, VT 05077; 802-889-3406

Tours: By appointment

President and head brewer Liz Trott is very excited about running the only women-owned and operated microbrewery in Vermont. With partner Janice Moran, Trott turns out five Tunbridge Quality Ales on a four-barrel Horeca system, built in Montreal by Pierre Rajotte. A home-brewer for fifteen years before going "pro," Trott hasn't yet been able to give up her day job, but she says that she enjoys her work as a senior citizens' advocate.

The Beer: Trott and Moran produce Telemark Mild, a traditional British mild ale; Covered Bridge IPA; and Ox Pull Stout. World's Fair Special, named after the local agricultural fair, will change from year to year; the 1996 version was a Flemish ale. Liz Trott's favorite is her Sap Brew, available in the spring. Made by replacing the water with pure maple syrup, it is brewed in the style of a blond ale.

Area Attractions: Liz Trott suggests that since North Tunbridge is just about dead-center in Vermont, many activities are only a half-hour away. The Woodstock and Mad River Glen ski areas and Dartmouth College are a short jaunt from Jigger Hill.

Long Trail Brewing Company (formerly Mountain Brewers)
P.O. Box 168; U.S. Route 4; Bridgewater Corners, VT 05035; 802-672-5011

Tours: Call for information

Gift shop: Open from 10 A.M. to 6 P.M.

Complimentary tastings: 12 noon to 5 P.M. daily.

Mountain Brewers founder and president Andy Pherson explains why the company, which opened in 1989, has changed its name: "Our Long Trail beers are better known than we are, and for years that's how most people have referred to us. We're just making it formal."

The name change accompanied a move from leased basement space in the Bridgewater Mill to a nine-acre riverside parcel

Long Trail Brewing company's home on the banks of the Ottauquechee River.

of land and a 15,000-square-foot brewery.

The new facility offers improved brewing productivity, lab-analysis capability, shipping and receiving efficiency, administration, and information management. A visitors center showcases the brewery's products, provides guided tours, and sells gifts and beer to go.

Production Manager Matthew Quinlan checks the carbonation level of a batch of Long Trail Ale.

The company is located between Killington and Woodstock on U.S. Route 4, a thirty-minute drive west of Exit 1 on I-89, and a fifteen-minute drive from the junction of State Route 100 and U.S. Route 4.

Correspondent Paul Kowalski reports that Long Trail beers are served in many local restaurants. Call for a list if you can't make it to the brewery.

Madison Brewing Company Pub and Restaurant

428 Main Street; Bennington, VT 05201; 802-442-7397

An interesting menu combines with friendly staff and designer decor to bring Bennington its first brewery restaurant. Owned and run by the Madison family—Mark, Mel, Mike, and their parents—this establishment offers some of the most interesting entrées I've seen in a "pub."

The Beer: Mark Madison, who trained at Shipyard Brewing Company, is the brewmaster and serves up Monument Golden, Crowtown Pale, Olde 76 Strong Ale, Willoughby's Scottish Ale, Battlefield Stout, and a raspberry stout.

The Food: The diverse menu offers surf-and-turf, featuring four large shrimp served with a garlic cream sauce; shrimp scampi over linguine;

seafood Alfredo; roast pork tenderloin; Delmonico steak; and veggie stir fry. There are four different varieties of bratwurst and bangers, all soaked in beer; lamb stew; Madison's meatloaf; and beer-battered fish and chips. Add interesting salads, sandwiches, appetizers, and homemade corn bread and boule, and you have good reason to include Bennington in your Vermont trek.

Area Attractions: Call the Bennington Area Chamber of Commerce at 802-447-3311.

Magic Hat Brewing Company
180 Flynn Avenue; Burlington, VT 05401; 802-658-2739

The Magic Hat folks have their beers brewed under contract, but will soon brew their own. Call ahead to ask about touring their new Burlington facility, due to open in late 1997.

The Beer: Magic Hat beers include: Magic Hat Ale, Blind Faith, and #9, described as a "Not Quite Pale Ale."

McNeill's Brewery
90 Elliot Street; P.O. Box 98; Brattleboro, VT 05301; 802-254-2553

Tours: Friday, Saturday, and Sunday at 2 P.M.

Gift shop: T-shirts, bar towels, and glasses are available at the bar from 4 P.M. to 1 A.M.

E-mail address: mbrew@sover.net

Ray McNeill and his wife, Holiday, celebrated their pub's tenth anniversary in 1996. It's a hands-down favorite among my Internet friends, who say visiting McNeill's is a must if you're traveling to Vermont. Dave Lyons: "The food is okay. What is

Owner/brewer Ray McNeill takes a break.

great is the beer. It's the only brewpub I would drive more than fifty miles for." Larry Williams: "I loved the Dead Horse and Duck's Breath." Ardis Osborne: "My son says that McNeill's ten to twelve brews are all good."

The Beer: Kerry Byrne of *Yankee Brew News* says of McNeill's, "There's only one thing wrong with this place; sooner or later, you have to leave." And *Ale Street News* columnist Peter Terhune raved about Ray McNeill's Old Ringworm Strong Ale, tasted with fellow beer judges in a blind test: ". . . elicited raves all around . . . very warming . . . long, deep maltiness . . . it's sexy . . ."

Ray's other beers are Alle Tage Altbier, a 1995 gold-medal winner at the Great American Beer Festival (GABF) in the German brown ale category; Big Nose Blond Ale, 1994 bronze-medal winner at the GABF in the golden ale category; Pullman's Porter, honorable mention at the 1995 GABF; Champale; Dead Horse IPA; Firehouse Amber; Exterminator Doppelbok; Old Ringworm; Oatmeal Stout; and Bucksnort Barley Wine. McNeill makes twenty-five varieties a year; nine of them are available in stores year-round. Or, try them at Redbone's in Somerville, Massachusetts.

The Food: My Internet gang loved the beer but mentioned that the food is just okay. Holiday McNeill stressed to me that the beer's the thing at McNeill's. She wouldn't send a menu or recipes. Since the pub doesn't open until 4 P.M., a trip to Brattleboro could begin with lunch at nearby Latchis Grille at 6 Flat Street, which seems to take the opposite approach —food over beer. You could then trek the couple of blocks to McNeill's to taste its brews.

Otter Creek Brewing Company

85 Exchange Street; Middlebury, VT 05753; 802-388-0727

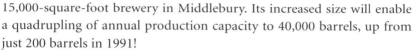

Tours: Fridays at 4 P.M. and 5 P.M., and Saturdays at 1 P.M., 3 P.M., and 5 P.M.

Dave Ebner, vice president of marketing for Otter Creek, is very proud of the company's new 15,000-square-foot brewery in Middlebury. Its increased size will enable a quadrupling of annual production capacity to 40,000 barrels, up from just 200 barrels in 1991!

The Beer: Otter Creek's beers are Copper Ale and Helles Alt Beer, which will be accompanied by a series of seasonals: Hickory Switch Smoked Amber Ale will be offered in the fall, while Stovepipe Porter will be served in the winter; Bock Spring Ale and Summer Wheat Ale will complete the lineup.

Area Attractions:

- **Middlebury's historic buildings** are a virtual history of Vermont and its architecture. Walking-tour maps are available by calling the Addison County Chamber of Commerce at 802-388-7951.

- **University of Vermont Morgan Horse Farm**
  RD #1, Box 196; Middlebury, VT 05753; 802-388-2011
  Hours: Open May through October; seven days a week. Call ahead for times as schedules change frequently.

  The Morgan horse is the state animal of Vermont, and a visit here is a chance to see a working farm dedicated to America's first breed of horse. After a guided tour, visitors are allowed to wander. This is a must for kids.

Ruben James Restaurant and Brewery

159 Main Street; Burlington, VT 05401; 802-864-0744

Hours: Sunday through Friday, from 11 A.M. to 2:30 A.M. Saturday from 11 A.M. to 1:30 A.M.

This casual eatery caters mostly to the local college crowd, offering live entertainment on weekends and a dance floor. Brewer Dean Martin, winner of several local home-brew competitions, stays creative with his beers, changing styles and names with each new batch. Ruben's Red Ale has proven to be one of his customers' favorites. The bar offers thirteen other microbrews on draft. The menu is inexpensive and includes burgers, chicken, pasta, and Mexican dishes.

The Shed Restaurant and Brewery

1859 Mountain Road; Stowe, VT 05672; 802-253-4364

Tours: To be announced.

Gift shop: A merchandise display case in the lobby of the main restaurant stocks retail goods that can be purchased during regular business hours.

In 1995, then-head brewer Chris Ericson took time out from a busy Saturday afternoon to show me around the

year-old brewery at the thirty-year-old Shed Restaurant. This Stowe institution had just reopened after renovations repaired damage from a 1994 fire. One of forty-three restaurants in this town of 3,000 residents, The Shed was packed that afternoon, indicating a healthy tourist economy.

The Beer: Already taxing the limits of its one-year-old, seven-barrel Peter Austin system, The Shed was cranking out four brews a week in 1995 to supply the pub and other locations demanding more and more of brewer Ericson's beer. At this writing, The Shed's brews were being distributed to twenty-eight restaurants and liquor stores, and expansion possibilities were being discussed. The list of popular beers includes Mountain Ale, which was making a big hit at the newly

opened Three Needs Brewpub in Burlington; West Branch Golden; Shed Amber Ale; Bruce Trail IPA; Phoenix Brown Ale; Raspberry Wheat Ale; Pumpkin Ale; Porter; Black Sheep Stout; and Sugarhouse Ale.

Head brewer Chris Ericson.

The Food: The Shed is known for its Shedburgers, created by owners Ken Strong and Ted Ross, the two ski instructors who opened the restaurant in 1965. The menu has been expanded greatly since those early days of simple burgers, steaks, and salads. Low-fat selections are marked by a tiny heart-shaped icon, and other items are asterisked to indicate the possibility of healthy alterations, such as leaving out the bacon, peanuts, cheese, etc.

So, if you're bloated by pub fare by the time you reach Stowe, give your arteries a break and try bruschetta; shrimp cocktail; Asian chicken-breast salad; fresh-fruit platter; grilled chicken-breast sandwich; Asian stir-fry noodles with julienned vegetables; vegetarian chili; vegetable-salad sandwich; "Chicken Mr. White" (strips of chicken breast, lightly sautéed with pineapple, almonds, and a garlic-and-soy sauce); and vegetarian pasta.

If you've been good all along, or just don't give a darn, venture into The Shed's regular menu for an onion flower, breaded and fried; buffalo wings; nachos; a sampler of shrimp tempura, potato skins, smoked ribs, and wings; chicken fajitas; roast duck Vermont; Jamaican jerk chicken; New York sirloin; prime rib; a seafood platter; baked, stuffed shrimp; and other high- and low-fat meals.

Area Attractions: Ericson was quick to point out that Stowe was a summer retreat a hundred years before the ski industry overtook the mountain. Summer is just as chock-full of events as winter. If you're not a skier, consider traveling to Stowe in the warm weather. There are more than a half-dozen golf courses in the area, an alpine slide, gondola rides, and in-line skating, as well as many other events and activities. Call 802-888-7300 for a Stowe Pocket Guide, featuring color photos, maps, phone numbers, and a year-round calendar of goings-on.

Three Needs Taproom and Brewery
207 College Street; Burlington, VT 05401; 802-658-0889

Trout River Brewing Company
Route 114; P. O. Box 360; East Burke, VT 05832; 802-626-3984

Hours: Closed Tuesdays; otherwise from 12 P.M. to 7 P.M. Open Fridays and Saturdays from 12 P.M. to 8 P.M. Sunday hours are 1 P.M. to 5 P.M.

Tours: During business hours and by appointment.

Co-owner Dan Gate has won a gold medal in the Scottish Ale category at one of the American Homebrewers Association's national competitions. His wife and partner, Laura, comments, "I get to wear about fifteen different hats here, and I like running our own business. I've found that I have to devote six days a month to completing the ridiculous amount of paperwork necessary to operating a microbrewery."

The Beer: The Gates produce Porter, Scottish Ale, Rainbow Red Ale, and Oktoberfest.

Area Attractions: Laura Gate recommends Burke Mountain, just two miles away, as a great ski resort for families. Trout River is also located on the Vast Trail, a snowmobiling trail of 200 to 300 miles. This translates into biking trails in the summer and spectacular foliage in the fall.

The Vermont Pub and Brewery
144 College Street; Burlington, VT 05401;
802-865-0500

Tours: Wednesdays at 8 P.M., Saturdays at 4 P.M., or by appointment.

If you're traveling to Vermont, you have to try Greg Noonan's place. He is well-respected

in the industry as a brewer dedicated to making great beer. Noonan himself gave me a tour of the brewery, which is located on the floor below the restaurant and bar. He pointed out that one of his recent beers, Thetford Red, was made with Vermont-grown hops and speculated that this local farm crop—

KATE CONE

killed more than a hundred years ago by Prohibition— just might make a comeback. Service in the pub was a bit brusque, and I was disappointed that Noonan didn't have time to chat with us about the beer. But, other customers seemed to be enjoying their experience.

The Beer: Just a portion of Greg Noonan's huge beer list includes Burly Irish Ale, Dogbite Bitter, Vermont Smoked Porter, Beetlejuice, Billybuck Maybock, Vermont Maple Ale, Wee Heavy 120 Shilling Ale, Kellerbier Lager, Grand Slam Baseball Beer, Joe Light, O'Fest (traditional Munich-style Oktoberfest lager), Black Bear Dunkerlager, Dunkel Weiss, Bohemian Lager, and Rock Dunder Brown Ale (a toasty Scottish brown ale). An entire menu of seasonals rotates throughout the year.

The Original BURLY RED IRISH ALE

The Food: The menu is very similar to that at the Seven Barrel Brewery, which is also owned by Noonan (see page 39). Soups, chili, salads, burgers, nachos, wings, and sandwiches share billing with more specialized dishes such as: smoked-salmon paté appetizer; raspberry teriyaki chicken; whisky steak; and traditional pub dishes like toad-in-the-hole, Cornish pastie, Welsh rarebit, a bratwurst dinner, shepherd's pie, and bangers and mash.

Windham Brewery at the Latchis Grille
The Latchis Hotel

6 Flat Street; Brattleboro, VT 05301; 802-254-4747

Tours: By appointment

Internet access: http://www.brattleboro.com/latchis

Hours: Dinner is served Wednesday through Sunday; lunch is available only on Friday, Saturday, and Sunday; the restaurant is closed all day Monday and Tuesday.

Located in the art deco-period Latchis Hotel in downtown Brattleboro is the Windham Brewery, which makes "honest ales, porters, and lagers" for the Latchis Grille.

The Beer: I walked through the brewery with then-head brewer Dan Young, who was planning to open his own brewpub in Greenfield, Massachusetts, soon. The brewing system at Windham Brewery is a homemade one, employing a fermenting tank that formerly simmered soup at the Campbell's plant in New Jersey. Beers are available for purchase in half-gallon growlers and, of course, at the Grille. Whetstone Lager, Moonbeam Ale, and Specialty Porter are the beers we tried.

The Food: The restaurant's menu is varied and interesting; prices range from $2.50 for a house salad to $17.00 for a grilled filet mignon, flamed in bourbon, with sherried Portobello mushrooms and a red-pepper-and-Roquefort butter, served over colcannon.

In between, one can dine moderately, in terms of both portions and price, with "Cafe Specials" like roasted-red-pepper kebbee; Tibetan momas (steamed lamb-and-pork dumplings with Asian hot sauce); sweet-potato tamales with orange-honey butter; spicy shrimp tamales; nachos grandes; spicy potato pancakes; chicken quesadillas; gravlax bruschetta; crab and shrimp over polenta; fried calamari; and varied focaccia pizzas. These items run from $5.00 to $9.00; soups and salads are available, also.

Dinner entrées include a paillard of chicken (thin breast of chicken, stuffed with orange, walnuts, and olives, then drizzled with hot basil oil and served over black-currant couscous); grilled fish of the day; fried chicken (boneless and skinless breasts that are breaded, deep fried, and served with mashed potatoes, gravy, and vegetables); "Knock and Brat" (premium knockwurst and bratwurst with beer bread, sauerkraut, and pickles); fish and chips made with lime brew-batter; a grilled pork chop served with comfort-food fixings; baked scrod; "Brewburgers," and daily specials. Prices range from $6.00 to the $17.00 filet mignon, with an average of $9.00.

In addition to the food, there's live jazz on Wednesday, Thursday, and Friday nights at 8:30 P.M. And, right in the same Latchis Hotel is the Latchis Theatre, where you can catch one of five movie choices after your dinner. On Tuesday and Wednesday nights, a "Hollywood and Dine" special provides dinner for two with beer (or wine), salad, and tickets to the theater for $31.99.

MASSACHUSETTS

In Massachusetts there are five areas where several microbreweries/
brewpubs are in relatively close proximity. These groupings are given
below, along with a consolidated list of area attractions that are also worth
a visit.

BOSTON AREA

Atlantic Coast Brewing (see page 74)
Back Bay Brewing Company (see page 75)
Boston Beer Company (see page 79)
Boston Beer Works (see page 81)
brew moon (see page 85)
Commonwealth Brewing Company (see page 93)
Fort Hill Brewhouse (see page 95)
Mass Bay Brewing Company (see page 100)
North East Brewing Company (see page 103)

AREA ATTRACTIONS

"Boston. America's Walking City" is the new slogan used by the Greater
Boston Convention and Visitors Bureau. If you're in town, and have the time,
you might as well see the sights. The following places of interest are suggested by the bureau. Call the staff at 800-374-7400 for more information. If
you're traveling with children, take the kids to the following must-sees:

• **New England Aquarium**
   Central Wharf; Milk Street and Atlantic Avenue;
   Boston, MA 02110; 617-973-5200
   T-stop: Blue Line at Aquarium
   Internet access: http://www.neaq.org//
   Located on Central Wharf at the intersection of Atlantic Avenue and
   Milk Street, the aquarium houses many continuing exhibits, plus an
   incredible spiral pedestrian ramp that rises up around the tall, cylin-
   drical fish tank in the center of the building. In the adjacent con-
   verted barge there is a sea lion show, featuring the talented Tyler (this

event is included in the initial ticket price). (Based on personal experience, I suggest doing this trip before imbibing, though if you think you can handle the lead-footed sensation as you lean into the upward climb of the ramp, while simultaneously looking down several dozen feet to the penguin tank, go ahead and try it.)

• **Museum of Science**
Science Park (off Memorial Drive); Boston, MA 02114; 617-723-2500
T-stop: Green line "E" train (Lechmere Line) to Science Park
Internet access: http://www.mos.org/
The current Museum of Science had its beginnings as far back as 1830, when six men established the Boston Society of Natural History at the corner of Berkeley and Boylston Streets in the Back Bay. In 1951, the first wing of the science museum opened at the current Cambridge location—on land leased for ninety-nine years from the Metropolitan District Commission. The Museum of Science now boasts more than 400 interactive exhibits for 1.6 million visitors a year. Begun by men, the museum now has a children's exhibit called "Women in Science," celebrating the contributions women have made to science over the centuries.

Among the most popular exhibits are the virtual-reality and live-animal programs, the Hayden Planetarium and "Lightning!" which uses the world's largest generator to produce artificial lightning bolts up to fifteen feet long. During the program, the cage in which the demonstrator sits is struck by 1.5 million volts to show why cars are safe during lightning storms.

• **The Computer Museum**
300 Congress Street; Boston, MA 02115; 617-426-2800
T-stop: Red line to South Station
Internet access: http://www.tcm.org/index.html
The Computer Museum features more than 170 interactive exhibits including "The Networked Planet," a new gallery on the Information Highway; the award-winning "Walk-Through Computer 2000," a multimedia robot show; and one of the most extensive collections of

historical computers and robots in the world. Close by is the Boston Tea Party Ship and Museum, on the Congress Street Bridge.

Take in the nearby historical sites.

• **USS Constitution**

Pier 1, Charlestown Navy Yard; P.O. Box 1812; Charlestown, MA 02129; 800-374-7400 (enter speed-select code *175 after call is answered)

T-stop: Green line to Haymarket, then buses #92 and 93

Orange line to Sullivan, then buses #92 and 93

Old Ironsides is the oldest commissioned warship afloat anywhere in the world.

• **Bunker Hill Pavilion (Seasonal)**

55 Constitution Road; Charlestown, MA 02129; 617-241-7575

The pavilion offers a striking multimedia recreation of the Battle of Bunker Hill.

• **Bunker Hill Monument**

Monument Square; Charlestown, MA 02129; 617-242-5641

This is the site of the pivotal June 17, 1775, Battle of Bunker Hill.

CAMBRIDGE AREA

Harvard Square: brew moon (see page 85)

John Harvard's Brew House (see page 96)

Kendall Square: Cambridge Brewing Company (see page 90)

AREA ATTRACTIONS

• **The Sports Museum of New England**

100 CambridgeSide Place (at the CambridgeSide Galleria); Cambridge, MA 02141; 617-57-SPORT

Near the Museum of Science is this tribute to New England sports and athletes. Begun by Celtics star Dave Cowens, the one-of-a-kind museum is "not just a gawker's paradise," according to *Boston Globe* columnist Bob Ryan. The museum contains more than the usual: exhibits on rowing, racing and bowling, as well as the Boston Marathon; a display featuring Paul Newman's race car; a virtual-reality exhibit where you become Roger Clemens' catcher; and Stump Haggerty, a computer with which you can match trivia wits. The museum store offers lots of clothing, gear, and souvenirs, including collector's items.

- **Massachusetts Institute of Technology Museum**
  265 Massachusetts Avenue; Cambridge, MA 02139;
  617-253-4444 (recorded information)
  Internet access: http://web.mit.edu/museum/html
  Hours: Tuesday through Friday, from 9 A.M. to 5 P.M. (opens at 10 A.M. beginning December 1); Saturday and Sunday, from 12 noon to 5 P.M.
  Admission: $3.00; senior citizens, children under twelve, $1.00

The museum, is just a few blocks away from Cambridge Brewing Company. You should phone for a complete list of exhibitions, but the facility's web page piqued my interest with "Schooners and Whalers: Watercolors by Benjamin Russell" and the "Hall of Hacks," a place that memorializes all the practical jokes played by MIT students over the decades. Officially, a "hack" involves mastery of wit and/or engineering technique, and memorable examples here range from snow-making in the dormitories to turbojets in the lecture halls. Also on display are a talcum-filled weather balloon that exploded on the field during the 1982 Harvard/Yale football game; the original "Nerd Crossing" sign that was erected along Memorial Drive to alert speeding motorists to the presence of MIT students in need of safe passage; and the centerpiece of the exhibition: a police car (complete with flashing lights, a lifelike dummy policewoman, and a box of half-eaten donuts) that students placed on top of the Great Dome in May 1994.

A real jewel, and one for the entire family, is the exhibit of holography, the art/science of three-dimensional imaging. Formerly housed at the Museum of Holography in New York, this largest and most comprehensive of hologram collections was acquired by MIT in January 1993. Using more than 70 of the 1,500 pieces in the collection, the exhibit looks at three facets of holography: the artistic, technical, and historical.

CAPE COD & THE ISLANDS

Hyannis: Cape Cod Brew House (see page 92)
Martha's Vineyard: The Brewery on Martha's Vineyard (see page 84)
Nantucket: Cisco Brewers (see page 93)

AREA ATTRACTIONS

This is a great place for people-watching. Randy Hudson says many of the Hollywood glitterati vacation on the island. You can catch Danny DeVito, Billy Joel, John Mellencamp, or Michelle Pfeiffer. For the more cultured and refined, there's plenty to do:

• **Nantucket Historical Association**
  Nantucket, MA 02554; 508-228-1894
  For one fee, you can tour several distinctive historical sites, including Greater Light, the Hadwen House, the Jethro Coffin House, and the Old Gaol (the first U.S. prison that allowed inmates to go home at night. Also on your list should be the Old Mill, where 1746 machinery still grinds corn with wind power, and the Whaling Museum, where you can see relics from the island's whaling past. Call for tour times and prices.

• **The Loines Observatory**
  Milt Street Extension; Nantucket, MA 02554; 508-228-9273
  The observatory offers children's astronomy classes, talks by astronomers, and other public programs.

IPSWICH AREA

Dornbush Brewing Company (see page 94)
Ipswich Brewing Company (see page 95)

AREA ATTRACTIONS

Located 35 miles north of Boston, Ipswich is typical of many coastal New England towns, having both historical attractions as well as miles of beautiful beaches. A few of the offerings are:

- **Crane's Beach**
  Argilla Road; Ipswich, MA 01938; 508-356-4354
  Winter or summer, this four miles of white-sand beach and dunes has marked trails for hiking, and there's an annual sandcastle competition in August.
- **Ipswich River Wildlife Sanctuary**
  87 Perkins Row; Topsfield, MA 01983; 508-887-9264
  The Massachusetts Audubon Society maintains this 2,800-acre sanctuary, offering ten miles of walking trails, opportunities for bird observation, and canoeing.
- **Candlewood Golf Club**
  75 Essex Road; Ipswich, MA 01938; 508-356-2398
  Located on Route 133, this course features nine holes and a greens fee of $7 to $10.
- **The Clam Box of Ipswich**
  Route 1A, 246 High Street; Ipswich, MA 01938; 508-356-9707
  For sixty years, the Clam Box has been frying up the plump, luscious mollusks for ravenous patrons.
- **Goodale Orchards Winery**
  143 Argilla Road; Ipswich, MA 01938; 508-356-5366
  Tours and samples are available on a seasonal basis.
- **Historic Walking Tour**
  Armed with a guide from the Ipswich Visitor's Center (available by calling 508-356-4400), you can stroll the town green and view the largest collection of pre-1725 homes in the country, including First Period, Second Period, Georgian, Federal, and Victorian houses.
- **Castle Hill**
  290 Argilla Road; Ipswich, MA 01938; 508-356-4351
  This fifty-nine-room Georgian mansion was built by Chicago businessman Richard Crane in 1927. Castle Hill overlooks Crane's Beach and is open for tours and picnicking; in the summer, it offers outdoor concerts, barn concerts, and a Fourth of July celebration.

WESTERN MASSACHUSETTS/BERKSHIRES

Great Barrington: Barrington Brewery & Restaurant (see page 77)
Holyoke: Paper City Brewing Company (see page 108)
Northhampton: Northhampton Brewery (see page 103)
Pittsfield: The Brewery at 34 Depot Street (see page 82)
South Deerfield: Berkshire Brewing Company (see page 78)
Springfield: Pioneer Valley Brewpub (see page 109)

AREA ATTRACTIONS

Again, you're in the heavenly Berkshires. There's skiing at Catamount and Butternut peaks, foliage in fall, the music at Tanglewood in the summer, and—for some modicum of normalcy—the Norman Rockwell Museum.

- **Historic Deerfield**
  The Street (off Routes 5 and 10); Deerfield, MA 01342; 413-774-5581
  Visit any of fourteen museum/houses; delve into Deerfield history and culture, and early-American decorative arts; and take a scenic meadow walk.
- **Children's Museum at Holyoke**
  444 Dwight Street; Holyoke, MA 01040; 413-536-KIDS
  Located about 20 miles south of South Deerfield, the museum features lots of hands-on exhibits.
- **Boston Symphony Orchestra**
  Tanglewood Music Festival (seasonal); Route 183; Lenox, MA 01240; 800-274-8499 (off season: 617-266-1492)
  The Berkshires are the summer home of the Boston Symphony Orchestra. Watch and hear them perform in this spectacular outdoor setting.
- **Jacob's Pillow Dance Festival (seasonal)**
  Box 287; Lee, MA 01238; 413-243-0745
  These performances of ballet, as well as modern, jazz, and traditional dance, feature talent from all over the world.

SKIING

- **Bousquet Ski Area**
  Dan Fox Drive, Pittsfield, MA, 413-442-8316

- **Brodie**
  Route 7, New Ashford, MA, 413-443-4752
- **Butternut Basin**
  Route 23, Great Barrington, MA, 800-438-SNOW
- **Catamount**
  Route 23, South Egremont, MA, 413-528-1262
- **Jiminy Peak**
  Corey Road, Hancock, MA, 413-738-5500
- **Otis Ridge**
  Route 23 West, Otis, MA, 413-269-4444

FOLIAGE (best between October 1 and 14)

Try Route 7 North, from Sheffield to Williamstown; Route 8, from Sandisfield to Dalton; and Route 183 from Great Barrington to Lenox.

BEER FESTIVALS

If you happen to be slogging through in the spring, catch the Berkshire County Brewer's Festival in late March. The Brewery at 34 Depot Street hosted this event in 1996.

Partake of the ripple effect of Smith College's cultural offerings.

- **Smith College Museum of Art**
  Bedford Terrace at Elm Street; Northampton, MA 01060; 413-585-2760
  Boasting a collection of more than 24,000 works of art, with the focus on nineteenth- and twentieth-century American and European painting, the museum also offers tours, gallery talks, lectures, and films at different times during the year.
- **Northampton Center for the Arts**
  17 New South Street; Northampton, MA 01060; 413-584-7327
  Watch performances of New England-based theater and dance troupes, and enjoy art exhibits.
- **Calvin Coolidge Memorial Room**
  Forbes Library; 20 West Street; Northampton, MA 01060; 413-584-6037
  Political animals and Calvin Coolidge fans, take heed. This room

at the Forbes Library contains some of Northampton resident Coolidge's public papers, speeches, and presidential memorabilia.

• **Look Memorial Park**

   413-584-5457

   Bordering the Mill River, Look Park features 200 acres of walking or jogging paths, tennis courts, picnic areas, a petting zoo, an amphitheater and a miniature railroad.

• **Norwottuck Rail Trail**

   Bike along an 8½-mile trail that goes from Northampton to Amherst. Local bike shops will rent you wheels if you don't want to lug your own. Call the *Daily Hampshire Gazette* at 413-584-5000 for a brochure that describes the trail in more detail.

Atlantic Coast Brewing

50 Terminal Street; Boston, MA 02129 (Charlestown); 617-242-6464

Tours: Fridays from 4 P.M. to 6 P.M., or by appointment

   Gift shop: Open during tours

   E-mail: tremont@hnt.com

   Internet access: http://www.hnt.com/tremont/

   At the foot of Bunker Hill, less than two miles from downtown Boston, Atlantic Coast Brewing crews have been turning out their Tremont products since April 1994. The brewery claims to

be the first to introduce cask-conditioned ales to the Boston area.

The Beer: Labeled "The Best Little Brewhouse in Boston" in 1996 by *Yankee Brew News* publisher Don Gosselin, Atlantic Coast Brewing is growing by leaps

and bounds, pushing the limits of its twenty-barrel Peter Austin brewing system, which was installed by Shipyard's Alan Pugsley. Some of the brewery's products will be available in bottles by the time this book reaches print. Among Gosselin's favorites are: Tremont Old Scratch Barley Wine, Tremont Cask-Conditioned Ale, Tremont IPA, and Tremont ESB.

Brewer Jeff Biegert conducts a tour.

Back Bay Brewing Company
755 Boylston Street; Boston, MA 02116-2618; 617-424-8300

Sitting a short walk from the Copley Square stop of the Massachusetts Bay Transit Authority trains, directly across Boylston Street from the Prudential Center, Back Bay Brewing Company celebrated its debut on the

Boston brewpub scene in December 1995. Stunningly decorated, BBBC balances the incredible decor with friendly staff and a high-end menu befitting its Back Bay setting. It is highly recommended by my former

contract-law professor and fellow mystery writer Jeremiah F. Healy, and I concur with his rave review. On the day I visited, bartender Jimmy Galenti happily poured samplers, chatted with me about each beer, and described the warm reception Back Bay Brewing Company has enjoyed in the short time since its opening.

Mystery writer Jeremiah F. Healy relaxes at the bar.

The Beer: Head brewer Tod Mott has divided his duties between Commonwealth Brewing Company and BBBC, where he oversaw the installation of the fifteen-barrel DME brewing system. Mott is quick to state that the beer recipes at BBBC are brand new, no repeats of the Commonwealth brews. In addition to the four beers mentioned below, Mott will serve a Russian Imperial Stout, an IPA and a German lager.

The Food: Reading the menu can bring tears to your eyes, simply because you know that you can't possibly try every single dish in one visit. They all cry out to be sampled. Appetizers, or "tapas," range from $4.25 for "Hearty Winter Greens" with toasted-herb croutons and red-ale dressing, to $7.95 for the warm lobster spring roll with Thai basil sauce, or the orange and coriander-battered shrimp with apricot dipping sauce. A meal could be made just with a few of these gems, served with a sampler of Back Bay's beers.

Entrées run from $9.95 for fusille with hardwood-grilled chicken breast in a light, wild-mushroom cream sauce to $22.95 for veal porterhouse with autumn-vegetable timbale and Roquefort veal jus. Other mouth-watering items are: grilled calamari with lemon/sage dressing and oven-dried tomato bruschetta; smoked corn and shrimp chowder with an English soda cracker; seared North Atlantic salmon with Ancho chili succotash; beef short ribs spiced with red curry, cumin, and cinnamon; and baby penne with veal-and-wild broccoli sausage, hot cherry peppers, oven-dried tomatoes, and extra-virgin olive oil.

Chef Ed Doyle, formerly of the Boston Harbor Hotel, is in charge of this ambitious kitchen. He gets together with Back Bay's brewer to create what they call the "Brewer's Winter Menu," pairing the company's beers with seasonal specialties. For $32.00 per person, loosen your belt for wild-mushroom ravioli with house-smoked bacon and French beans, served with Arlington Amber; Frisse and grilled pears with Stilton and spiced walnuts, served with Boylston Bitter; a choice of hickory-roasted rack of lamb with horseradish potato crisp and Brussels sprouts, or grilled striped bass with oven-dried tomato and scallion risotto, both served with Freedom Trail Pale Ale. And for dessert, chocolate porter mousse with almond pretzels is served with Park Square Porter.

Non-beer drinkers can splurge on Back Bay's dessert sampler: hazelnut meringue crisp, toasted pound cake, and chocolate mousse mug. Then, they can head across the street to the Top of the Hub (or across Copley Square to the John Hancock Building) and peer through the telescopes at their loved one sipping beer at the Back Bay Brewing Company.

Barrington Brewery and Restaurant

Mailing address: 420 Stockbridge Road; Great Barrington, MA 01230
Street address: Rt. 7, Jenifer House Commons;
Great Barrington, MA 01230; 413-528-8282

Gary Happ is proud owner of Barrington Brewery and Restaurant, informing me in 1995 that summer business was "tremendous" and that the fall season was promising to be equally so. He cites his emphasis on good food as the main reason. "Some people think you can be successful by brewing a few unique beers and serving prepackaged food. That's just not so. You have to have a strong kitchen to start." Barrington pays attention to the details, making its own salad dressings, soups, and chilis. "We sell a lot of our specialty salads," says

Happ. "What's the point of putting together intriguing ingredients, then dumping bottled dressing over them?"

The Beer: Andre Mankin, Barrington's British-trained brewer, turns out Mohican Amber, Hopland Pale Ale, and Black Bear Stout using a seven-barrel system. Happ says that Mankin is always creating seasonals and will soon offer an Octoberfest, a best bitter, a porter, and an all-organic beer made with hops from Canada.

The Food: Try Happ's bestseller, the "Brewer's Salad": mixed greens, hard-boiled egg, roasted red peppers, tomato, bacon, and sprouts with either homemade shallot-herb, Russian, or blue-cheese dressings. Another winner is the "Brewer's Pocket": spinach, smoked turkey, bacon, sprouts, onion, and melted Swiss cheese, slathered with blue-cheese dressing. Other house specialties include house-made semolina/ale baguette, served with all salads and soups; cheddar/ale soup; a mixed-sausage appetizer; and stout-marinated steak, grilled, covered with mushrooms and onions, and served on garlic bread. On the "after five" menu, Happ also offers a design-your-own-pasta option, similar to the make-your-own-pizza concept popular elsewhere. For you pub-fare lovers, there is a shepherd's pie that sells like hotcakes, even in summer; a chef's pot pie du jour; New York strip steak; chicken quesadillas; bow-tie pasta with shrimp; and Southwest chicken breast.

Enjoy the food until the smoke-free dining room closes, then head upstairs to the game room, where you can shoot a few rounds of pool and light up that cigar you've been saving.

Berkshire Brewing Company

12 Railroad Street; South Deerfield, MA 01373-0096; 413-665-6600

Tours: Saturdays from 1 P.M. to 3 P.M. Special tours for groups on Friday nights, by appointment.

Gift shop: None. Brewmania is sold during tours.

Located by the rails in a 7,000-square-foot building that was originally a cigar manufacturing plant, Berkshire Brewing Company has garnered a whopping 200 draft accounts in western Massachusetts since its October 1994 opening.

Owners Chris Lalli, a former laser engineer, and Gary Bogoff, a building contractor, realized a five-year-long dream when they got their home-made seven-barrel system up and running. For their first anniversary party last October, Lalli and company roasted a pig, injecting it periodically with a mixture of their porter and with maple syrup. Now *that's* a recipe. Lalli also notes that the East Side Grill in nearby Northampton uses his beer to make its beer-and-cheddar soup.

The Beer: The company now produces Steel Rail Extra Pale Ale, Berkshire Ale, and Drayman's Porter. Come for a tour, then head over to the Yankee Candle Company restaurant and enjoy the brews, which are also sold in twenty-two-ounce bottles in the center of town, at D'Amaio's store.

Boston Beer Company/Samuel Adams - The Brewery

30 Germania Street; Boston, MA 02130 (Jamaica Plain); 617-522-3400

Tours: Thursdays at 2 P.M.; Saturdays at 12 noon and again at 2 P.M. There is a fee for admission to the facility. The suggested donation of $1.00 per person is given annually to a local organization; most recently the recipient is the Ford Hall Forum, an eighty-six-year-old Boston lecture series designed to provide an avenue for freedom of speech.

Gift shop: Yes

I already know what you're saying: "Sam Adams is not a microbrewed beer!"

The Samuel Adams Brew-house at the Lenox Hotel.

The first year Jim Koch intro-
duced his darling lager, he sold
7,000 barrels, clearly bringing
the company within the defini-
tion of a microbrewery. However, it was a contract beer made
by other breweries. And it's not
produced in New England,
unless you count the minuscule
amounts brewed in the Jamaica
Plain facility, opened in 1988.

But, you have to give the guy
credit. When he chucked his
high-paying management consultant's job in 1984 to make beer, he was
the first in New England to get his feet wet in the micro business. The reason people try the current, real microbrews is because Sam Adams
"greased the skids," so to speak, with its varied products, which, I might
remind you, have won many awards and medals in the decade-plus
they've been sold.

Mike LaCharite, owner and brewmaster at Casco Bay Brewing Company in Maine (see page 13) helps judge Boston Beer Company's annual
homebrewer's contest, and says its tour is a "must-do." You can visit two
locations in Boston: the brewery in Jamaica Plain or the pub on Boylston
Street in Back Bay. Now, I said in my introduction to this book that I
wasn't going to rate brewpubs, but I can't recommend going to the Sam
Adams pub. The staff is nice, but the place was clearly set up to give its
parent company some visibility in a tony area of the city. The beers are
available in samplers or pints, but no brewing is done on site. I overheard
the manager tell a salesperson that the Lenox Hotel, to which the pub is
"attached," bought the license to use the Sam Adams name for what is
basically the hotel bar. I would head over to the brewery, take the tour,
then come back to town to try Back Bay Brewing Company, a block away
and across Boylston Street from the Sam Adams facility.

Boston Beer Works
Slesar Brothers Brewing Company, Inc.

61 Brookline Avenue; Boston, MA 02215; 617-536-2337

Hours: 11:30 A.M. to 1 A.M., Sunday through Saturday
Tours: Saturday and Sunday at 2 P.M.
Gift shop: Retail goods are available at the host stand
T-stop: Green Line to Kenmore Square; walk up Brookline Avenue

Boston Beer Works is across from Fenway Park. Opened in 1992, this is the most casual of the Boston pubs, boasting an industrial-look decor and its proximity to the ballpark; on game nights, the place can be said to be "hopping." Both the beer and food menus are extensive, including—on the food side—soups, salads, burgers, sandwiches, grazing foods, pasta, and grilled items. Prices are moderate.

All of the Works' homemade desserts are listed with at least one house beer that complements the recipe. Examples include: Muddy River ice-cream pie with Beantown Nut Brown Ale or Muddy River Porter; apple/cinnamon/raisin pie with Fruit Beer or Cider; and chocolate-mousse cake with Kenmore Kolsch or Climax Wheat.

Internet friend Russell Mast, now of Chicago, visits Boston Beer Works every time he's in town, and gives it rave reviews. And, a certain Bath, Maine, dentist/beer judge/home-brewer I know says this is his favorite New England brewpub.

The Beer: Boston Beer Works' active beer list is three pages long and describes thirty-three different brews. The award winners are Hercules Strong Ale, which took the gold medal in the barley wine category at the 1994 Great American Beer Festival, and Centennial Alt, which was honored with a silver medal at the same event.

The Food: House specialties include Boston clam chowder or onion/ale soup; mako-shark sticks (skewered shark, tomatoes, and onions marinated in herbs and Raspberry Ale, then grilled); beer-batter onion rings; nachos; quesadillas; barbecue wings; hummus; and grilled veggies. Entrées include "Great Pumpkin Ravioli," tossed in a sherry/cream sauce and served with roasted acorn squash, red peppers, and basil—all topped with roasted pumpkin seeds; "Ragin' Cajun Jambalaya"; "Crusted Atlantic Salmon"; and, a grill favorite, the "Ultimate Works Combo," with steak tips, andouille sausage, baby back ribs, and boneless chicken breast.

The Brewery at 34 Depot Street

34 Depot Street; Pittsfield, MA 01201; 413-442-2072

Tours: Every Saturday; call for times

The Brewery at 34 Depot Street has been serving brewer Mike Merrill's beers since July 1994. Using a five-barrel Peter Austin brewing system, The Brewery prides itself on bringing back a piece of Pittsfield history: Prior to Prohibition, beer was made there by the Berkshire Brewing Company, considered to be one of the finest breweries in the Northeast.

The Beer: Continuing this tradition, Merrill's offerings include Gimlick's Golden Ale, Red Room Pale Ale, Irish Red Lenox Half Stock Ale, Iron Works India Pale Ale, and Ravens Rock Stout. Seasonal beers are also made here and visitors are urged to ask their server for the currently available specialties.

Other places that serve The Brewery's beers are Red Lion Inn, Stockbridge; Berkshire Hilton Inn, Pittsfield; Canterbury's Pub, Williamstown; Freight Yard Pub, North Adams; Bousquet Ski Area, Pittsfield. Merrill, who ran a home-brew store for five years in nearby New York before heading up The Brewery's beer-making operations, recommends the Berkshire Hilton Inn and the Red Lion Inn as wise picks for overnight stays.

The Food: The Brewery's menu is casual and bargain priced, featuring burgers, sandwiches, pizza, and pasta, as well as specialty entrées, appetizers, and salads. Check out these smartly named selections: the "Woodchuck Platter," with raw vegetables and dip; the "Depot Street Platter," with hot wings, chicken toes, brewery fries, and onion rings; the "Awesome Onion," a colossal onion dipped in beer batter, fried, and served with honey mustard/ale sauce; "Onion Ale Soup," with melted Swiss and Monterey jack cheese; and "ChowdA," served in a rye-bread bowl.

Patrons can watch brewing operations from the dining room at The Brewery.

Sandwiches include "Justin's Favorite," a beer-battered chicken breast served on a hard roll; "Vegetarian's Delite," with lettuce, tomatoes, onions, cucumbers, bell peppers, sprouts, and Swiss cheese on seven-grain bread with basil mayonnaise; and the "Madonna," a bare breast of chicken that is grilled and served on seven-grain bread with lettuce, tomatoes, and fat-free mayonnaise. Entrées are classic dishes with the Brewery's own spin: "Foghorn Leghorn," a chicken breast marinated in the Brewery's own Red Room Pale Ale and secret spices, then grilled (see recipe); and fajitas, steak or chicken, marinated in house beer and Mexican spices and served sizzling on a hot platter with peppers, onions, salsa, sour cream, and flour tortillas.

Chef Richard parted with recipes for these favorites:

Onion/Ale Soup

3 ounces whole butter	12 ounces water
1 pound sliced Spanish onions	2 ounces beef base
½ pound sliced red onions	2 ounces chicken base
1 tablespoon white sugar	2 cups Golden Ale
2 tablespoons flour	1 tablespoon basil

Step One: Melt butter and sauté onions until golden brown, then add sugar. (Note that it is important to allow the onions to brown. The most common mistake with onion soup is to add the liquid before the onions are caramelized.)

Step Two: Add flour and mix with onions until it cannot be seen.

Step Three: Add remaining ingredients and simmer one hour. If desired, float a crouton in the soup and top with melted cheese.

FOGHORN LEGHORN

6 boneless chicken breasts, pounded	1 tablespoon brown sugar
12 ounces dark beer	3 tablespoons Worcestershire Sauce
1 tablespoon lime juice	3 tablespoons soy sauce
½ medium garlic clove, chopped	2 tablespoons seasoned salt

Step One: Combine all ingredients and place chicken breasts in marinade for at least one hour.

Step Two: Grill over medium heat, turning often. (Note that chicken is easily burned because of the brown sugar; make sure the grill is not too hot.)

The Brewery on Martha's Vineyard

Oak Bluffs, MA 02557; 508-696-8400

Slated to open in November 1996, this micro should offer island visitors a refreshing place to quaff. Call ahead for more information, though, because the company has been promising to open for a few years without doing so.

The Brewhouse at Danvers

65 Newbury Street (Route 1 North); Danvers, MA 01923; 508-777-6666

Tours: Available for parties of ten or more if prearranged.

Pasta, burgers, and pizza have been the standard fare here, but at press time the menu was undergoing "profound" changes and will feature more interesting items. The Brewhouse offers a mug club with no waiting list and more than 300 members; the fine beers are made by one of Kennebunkport Brewing Company's original brewers. Fred Weseman offers an extremely popular Extra Special Bitter, Misery Island Stout, General Putnam's Pale Ale, and Pugsley's Pilsner—named after its creator, Alan Pugsley of Shipyard Brewing Company.

brew moon

115 Stuart Street, City Place;
Boston, MA 02116; 617-523-6467

Hours: Seven days a week, from 11:30 A.M. to 2 A.M.

Tours: Specially arranged in conjunction with Old Town Trolley (see page 106).

Gift shop: Retail items and gift certificates are available.

T-stop: Green Line at Boylston

Okay, I can do e.e. cummings—"let's live suddenly without thinking . . ." —and head to brew moon for a beer. The first brew moon enterprises facility opened in Boston's Theatre District in December 1994, the second in Saugus, on Route 1, in January 1996, and the third in Harvard Square in June 1996. With seven more planned for the East Coast by 1999, brew moon is a classic example of this tenet: If you are well capitalized, the sky's the limit. Given its ambitious—no, quantum—expansion plans, this company will soon be the largest microbrew/restaurant chain in New England.

Winner of my award for "Caring Most about Getting Back to the Beleaguered Travel-Guide Author," is brew moon principal Dan Feiner. He and I played phone tag for weeks, and he was the persistent one. Rarely have I heard an owner exhibit so much enthusiasm for a brewpub. "Read our napkin!" Dan urged, when I told him I had recently learned that historically women had been instrumental in bringing beer to the table, other than as waitresses. Within the inter-

BREW MOON PHOTO

esting narrative were these words: "In the middle ages, women known as brewsters were the primary makers of beer. Beer is a food of the spirit." Short, but sweet.

Led by Elliot Feiner, the Boston Chicken "magnate," these people are committed to bringing you great food and great beer in a way that suggests that they know exactly what they want to do and how they want to do it: with quality products and the personal attention usually given only by much smaller brewpubs.

The Beer: Director of Brewery Operations Tony Vieira began his intense learning career at the Anheuser-Busch pilot research center in St. Louis, Missouri. For three years there, Vieira brewed three fifteen-barrel batches a day, five days a week. In a recent "Brewer's Corner" in *Brew* magazine, Vieira described his experience: "We malted our own grains, we ran our own kilns, we milled and we mashed. We did all kinds of experiments with new ingredients, new mashing techniques, filtration studies, non-alcoholic brews, wheat brews, ales, lagers. You name it, we brewed it." Vieira is convinced however, that brewing is as much an art as it is a science. When a brewer realizes this and reaches the point where he or she combines the two in perfect balance, that individual is on the way to really knowing something about the brewing process.

Vieira has created the following moon-theme (lower-cased) beers: moonlight, a light ale aimed at the budding beer connoisseur; boston special reserve, brewed from 100 percent American two-row malt and hopped with 100 percent American hops, crafted to meet Germany's purity law, boston special reserve redefines the American pilsner; grasshopper, an amber India Pale Ale, rich in character and aggressively hopped; iron works ale, a copper-colored, medium-bodied amber with a smooth malt flavor; eclipse extra stout, a full-bodied stout, brewed from eight different malts and roasted barley (creamy and distinctive, eclipse offers a subtle hoppy character that is delicately balanced). Vieira also offers blends: partial eclipse, equal portions of eclipse extra stout and boston special reserve; half and half, a mixture of eclipse and grasshopper; black velvet, an equal mixture of eclipse and cider jack hard apple cider; and snake bite, equal parts ironworks ale and cider jack hard apple cider. The brew moon's non-alcoholic variety is rocket root beer.

The Food: In the year that brew moon has been serving its eclectic menu and moon-theme beers at the Stuart Street location, it has received national attention from *Bon Appetit* magazine as "One of the Country's Best New Restaurants" for 1995. Since the moon is situated across from the newly restored Wang Center, its director of culinary operations, Donald Chapelle, a graduate of the prestigious Culinary Institute of America, caters largely to the theater crowd. Chapelle and Brewer Tony Vieira strive to create an exciting menu that enhances the lively selection of robust beers.

There are mouth-watering starter plates like grilled shrimp with scallion pancakes or sesame-seared tuna; entrées such as roast rosemary chicken breast, shrimp étouffée, or charred herb-pepper-crusted sirloin; and irresistible desserts, including a cappuccino ice-cream sandwich or bronzed fruit tart. The moon also offers burgers (black angus with various toppings and cheeses, as well as a grain-and-veggie burger), sandwiches (ancho-rubbed, grilled chicken breast with sharp cheddar and spicy aioli, cold meatloaf, or grilled Portobello mushroom), salads (haymarket: with grilled chicken and onions, romano protato crouton, roasted garlic, balsamic vinaigrette), grilled pizzas, and crostini. An extensive and well-thought-out wine list, including sherry and port selections, is available for the non-beer drinkers among you.

When I visited brew moon for lunch I found the dining room full, and there was much bustling about by waitstaff and patrons. Nonetheless, my party of five enjoyed our experience there. I would say that brew moon is not a place for an intimate lunch or dinner, but our server, Jenny, laughed through all our antics, promptly filled our demands, and made the trip to brew moon truly pleasant.

The appetizers we ordered were of huge proportion. The garlic sausage and equally garlic-flavored mashed potato plate, is a rendition of a British Isles pub dish called "bangers and mash." The two fat sausages and hefty pile of potatoes was easily enough to fill a normal person or to provide everyone at the table with a taste. And the other dish, a sampler plate, gave the five of us more than a taste of tender ribs; savory, seven-spice chicken wings (the nice meaty portion); and scallion pancakes. A selection of the moon's beers complemented all courses.

Everyone will enjoy the desserts, listed on the menu as "splashdown." All freshly made at the moon are a fresh-fruit tart, brew moon pudding (steamed in pale ale and served with caramel sauce and vanilla-bean ice cream), a chocolate sampler "xtc" (a nutty brownie, steamed pudding, chocolate/hazelnut ice cream and sauces), and a brewer's root-beer float (made with the moon's own rocket root beer).

Since the restaurant is located across from the Wang Center, you can hit the moon either before the theater, for dinner, or afterwards for desserts and—of course—beer. There's also a jazz brunch on Sundays.

Donald Chappelle graciously shared with us the following recipes:

ALE-STEAMED ARTICHOKE STUFFED WITH VEGETABLE HASH

For the hash:

2 ounces oil	1 ounce tomato purée
½ onion, diced medium	2 ounces tomato concassée
2 cloves garlic, mashed	3 ounces white wine
½ green pepper, diced	1 tablespoon basil, fresh
½ red pepper, diced	3 tablespoons parsley, fresh
½ zucchini, diced	½ teaspoon dried oregano
1 cup mushrooms, diced	1½ cups Parmesan cheese

In a skillet (and not a pan of another type), sauté onions until translucent, then add garlic and peppers. Add zucchini and mushrooms, and sauté two minutes. Add tomato purée and concassée, finish with herbs, and deglaze with wine when necessary. Finish with Parmesan cheese. Do not burn. Simmer five minutes. Add parsley, and chill.

For the artichokes:

4 large, fresh California artichokes	¼ cup water
½ cup ale	1 teaspoon lemon juice
¼ cup olive oil	1 teaspoon flour

Clean out artichokes, and discard outer leaves. Dip into lemon water, and set aside until ready to cook. Braise, covered, in liquid for twelve minutes. Set aside artichokes, keeping them covered and warm. Serve warm. Reheat in microwave if necessary.

For the bacon:

Dice 2 slices of apple-smoked bacon into ⅛-inch segments, and fry until crisp.

For the bagna cauda:

½ cup olive oil	6 anchovy fillets, diced fine
2 ounces butter	1 lemon, juiced
4 cloves garlic, diced fine	

Add garlic and anchovies to all other ingredients, and simmer on low for ten minutes or until anchovies are dissolved.

Add hash to artichokes, garnish each plate with four asparagus spears, tomato concassée, ½ teaspoon bacon crisps, and frisée lettuce. Serve warm.

Note

As mentioned, there are already two other brew moon locations:

114 Broadway, Route 1; Saugus, MA 01906; 617-941-BREW, and
50 Church Street, Harvard Square; Cambridge, MA 02138; 617-499-2739

Praised by Peter Terhune in his *Ale Street News* column, the third brew moon, which opened in June 1996, continues the Boston and Saugus stores' success in what a local radio commentator calls "The Peoples' Republic of Cambridge." Terhune recommends the "cosmopolitan and vegetarian-bent" menu and the Roggan Alt, the Excaliber Imperial Pale Ale, and the Continental-style lager called Rosin dubh.

Cambridge Brewing Company

One Kendall Square; Cambridge, MA 02139; 617-494-1994

Hours: Open Monday through Friday. Lunch is served from 11:30 A.M. to 4:30 P.M, dinner hours are 4:30 to 10 P.M, and pizza is served until midnight. Saturday and Sunday hours are from noon to 1 A.M.

Gift shop: Retail items are available at the host stand.

T-stop: The Red Line at Kendall Square

Artist/bartender Lee Wolf's mural dominates Cambridge Brewing company's front room.

Just a few blocks from the Massachusetts Institute of Technology, Cambridge Brewing Company is celebrating its seventh year as "the Cambridge representative of the renaissance in brewing taking place in this country."

There's a mini-art gallery to enjoy right on the premises: Cambridge's own Lee Wolf, a part-time CBC bartender and full-time artist, created the huge mural that graces one entire wall of the bar area. Wolf, thirty-one, has illustrated for the *New Yorker, Rolling Stone,* and the *Saturday Evening Post,* as well as providing the cover art for the books-on-tape version of author Armistead Maupin's *Tales of the City* trilogy. The mural in question depicts many Boston-area politicos (like Ted Kennedy), celebrities, and sports heroes mingling with CBC staff and customers.

The Beers: CBC's beers have pleased the palates of Cantabridgians as well as garnered more official notice: the brewery's Belgian Tripel won the 1992 Great American Beer Festival gold medal in the specialty-ale category, and its Charles River Porter took the 1990 bronze in the porter group. Rounding out the beer selections are the standards: Regatta Golden Ale, Cambridge Amber, and Tall Tale Pale Ale.

Specialties include wheats, winter warmers, a pumpkin ale, IPA, bitters, brown ales, and the Belgian Tripel. Two 1995 seasonals were Bannatyne's

Scotch Ale, named after owner/brewmaster Phil Bannatyne, and Blunderbuss Barley-wine, which is 11 percent alcohol by volume and is described as being a deep orange-gold, aged in American oak, with a woody, vanilla, chardonnay character. CBC is proud to have brewed six batches of its pumpkin ale in '95 to keep up with demand.

Using a ten-barrel system, head brewer Darryl Goss, with Will Meyers, turns out about 2,400 barrels a year. The company now offers its beer in growlers to take out. For under ten dollars, patrons can enjoy the Golden, Amber, Pale Ale, or Porter at home.

The Food: In the newly redecorated "back room," you will bask in the womb-like warmth of salmon-pink walls boasting original art, and you'll be dazzled by the shining stainless-steel brewery equipment nearby. Enjoy "Pasta from Hell," made with black tiger shrimp and fresh lemon pepper tagliatelle, tossed with tropical fruit juices, snow peas, and "Inner Beauty" hot sauce; a paella of shrimp, mussels, chicken, sausage, tomatoes, peas, scallions, and saffron rice; burgers and sandwiches that come with a choice of fries, slaw, or southwestern corn salad and include the "Marrakesh Express" (roasted eggplant and red pepper, hummus, marinated red onion, and spinach on a fresh-baked onion dill roll); and roasted turkey breast with smoked gouda, onion, watercress, and mango chutney on French bread. The smoked-salmon salad with fresh spinach and feta cheese, tossed with roasted-coriander vinaigrette looks good, as do the brick-oven pizzas.

KATE CONE

Appetizers range in price from $1.95 to $5.95 and in style from the "grazing" variety, (fried-chicken bits, tortilla chips with CBC's own salsa, chili, onion rings, Cajun popcorn shrimp, and nachos) to more unusual offerings, such as shrimp-and-spinach quesedilla; "Brewer's Bruschetta," a garlic crostini topped with warm plum tomatoes, basil, and red onion; mussels steamed in beer, which are seasoned with aromatic vegetables, Italian parsley and garlic; a hummus platter, with hummus, tabouli, celery, carrots, cherry tomatoes, and pita bread; and baked goat cheese served with a tomato, basil, and roasted-garlic purée and herbed foccacia.

Cape Cod Brew House

720 Main Street; Hyannis, MA 02601; 617-775-4110

Tours: Daily; call for times.

Bob Melley has put fifteen years of restaurant experience and ardent brew-pub research into transplanting the concept to Cape Cod, whose very first brewpub is also in Hyannis. Keen on being part of the community, the Brew House annually invites thirty other New England micros to its parking lot for a charitable summer brewfest, and the company participates in the "Brew Open," a golf tournament whose proceeds are also donated to charity.

The Beer: Offerings include Chatham Light, Lighthouse Lager, Nantucket Red Ale, and Dakota Dark. All reflect the Brew House's philosophy of achieving "a perfect balance in the beer's aroma and flavor . . ."

The Food: The menu is varied, featuring many pub-type dishes—especially those you'd want to sample on the Cape. Clam chowder, seafood stew, and barbecued shrimp are appetizers that will satisfy seafood fans, while chili, nachos, New Orleans–style crab cakes, and an onion blossom will please pub-food lovers. Entrées include scrod, a broiled seafood platter, fish and chips, baby back ribs, sirloin tips, fajitas, and burritos. Sandwiches and gourmet pizzas round out the Brew House menu.

Cisco Brewing Company

P.O. Box 2928; Nantucket, MA 02584; 508-325-5929

Owner/brewer Randy Hudson has worked many jobs in order to eke out a living on the island of Nantucket, but waxing philosophical, Hudson maintains that each job has enhanced his current position of microbrewery owner. Coaching a high-school soccer team, baking bread, making wine, landscaping, and working in a shellfish-propagation lab were necessary prebrewing professions that Hudson says allowed him to live year-round on an island that comes alive with tourists for only a few months a year.

In business since July 1995, Hudson is already upgrading his equipment. He has purchased a seven-barrel brewing system from Ipswich Brewing Company and hopes this expansion will enable him to place his beers in every restaurant and bar on Nantucket. Then he'll think about "exporting" his products to the mainland.

Commonwealth Brewing Company

138 Portland Street; Boston, MA 02114; 617-523-8383

Tours: Specially arranged in conjunction with Old Town Trolley (see page 106)

T-stop: Green Line at North Station

Commonwealth Brewing Company began Boston's brewpub revolution in 1987. Joe Quattrocchi is the visionary owner of both Commonwealth and the new Back Bay Brewing Company (see page 75). Head Brewer Tod Mott continues to impress with Burton Ale and India Pale Ale, among others. The closest brewpub to the new Fleet Center, Commonwealth is the only place to go before or after a Bruins or Celtics game. It's just a short hike off Causeway Street until you see the gleaming copper kettles beckoning to you through the huge windows of this charming brick building, now on the National Historic Register.

Concord Junction Brewing Company

152 Commonwealth Avenue; West Concord, MA 01742; 508-371-9929

Internet access: http://www.tiac.net/users/cjbc/

Brewer Brett Pacheco talked with me by phone on Labor Day in 1996 and proudly touted his Concord-based joint venture with Jon Cahill. There are no holidays for this young brewer. Not yet. But industriousness, apropos for the town that helped launch our country's revolution, has paid off. Pacheco's Concord Pale Ale is being extremely well received. "Even our distributor was happily surprised," Pacheco says. If you're in town, ask for this brew at Walden Station Restaurant, where I once worked a second job as a waitperson. The place has great food and now great beer.

Area Attractions: Brett Pacheco recommends a visit to the Wine and Cheese Shop in Concord Center, right across the street from Walden Station. It has been around for ages and contains an eclectic selection of cookware, dishware, barware, wine and cheese, and other homemade take-home food.

Another Concord tradition is the five-and-dime store in West Concord center, near the brewery. This is an old-fashioned establishment reminiscent of the 1940s or 1950s; sadly, it lacks a soda fountain, but happily, it has aisles and aisles of quirky items you just can't do without.

Concord is a tourist attraction without a brewery, but Walden Pond, the Alcott House, and Ralph Waldo Emerson's homestead are all ready for history-hungry travelers. For more information, contact the Concord Area Chamber of Commerce at 508-369-3120.

Dornbusch Brewing Company

31 Mitchell Road; Ipswich, MA 01938; 508-356-0093

Horst Dornbusch makes the German-style beers of his homeland at Smuttynose Brewery in Portsmouth, New Hampshire, but is planning his own brewpub in Gloucester, Massachusetts. For now, you can reach him in Ipswich. Of his two creations, one—the Dornbusch Golden—is a Dortmund-style lager, and the other is a Dusseldorf Lagered Ale. These unique-to-New-England brews are available in twelve-ounce bottles at liquor stores and restaurants in Massachusetts, Pennsylvania, and New Jersey. Scheduled for a spring 1998 opening is The Gloucester Brewkettle and the Homebrew Fermenter Supply Store at 16 Rogers Street, Gloucester, MA 01930 (508-281-4411). Now under construction in one of the prettiest towns in Massachusetts, this facility features a pub and a seven-barrel brewing system. Dornbusch plans a winning combination of German- and British-style beers and cuisine that is sure to please. The pub will serve bratwurst, currywurst, rolladen, and sauerbraten, all accompanied by German-style potato salad and French fries. English items will include fish and chips, bangers and mash, steak-and-kidney pie, and shepherd's pie. In addition to his two existing styles, Dornbush will make an Alt, a Munich Pilsner, a black lager, and a wheat beer. On the Brit side will be a pale ale, an IPA, a stout, a porter, and several seasonals.

Fort Hill Brewhouse

125 Broad Street; Boston, MA 02110; 617-695-9700

Ipswich Brewing Company

23 Hayward Street; Ipswich, MA 01938; 508-356-3329

E-mail: jcb@ipswich.com

Internet access: http://www.ipswich.com

Tours: Saturdays at 1 P.M. and 3 P.M. (special group tours are available)

Since its grand opening in October 1992, Ipswich Brewing Company has increased in size thirteen-fold, producing Ipswich Ale, Ipswich Dark Ale, and Ipswich Oatmeal Stout, plus an annual seasonal brew. Sold in half-gallon growlers, which are sterilized and reused upon return, Ipswich brews can be found in liquor stores throughout Massachusetts and elsewhere in New England.

John Harvard's Brew House

33 Dunster Street, Harvard Square; Cambridge, MA 02138; 617-868-3585

Hours: Lunch is served Monday through Friday from 11:30 A.M. to 3:30 P.M.; on Saturday and Sunday, brunch is available from 11:30 A.M. to 3:30 P.M. Dinner is served Sunday through Wednesday from 5 P.M. to 10 P.M. and Thursday through Saturday from 5 P.M. to 11 P.M. The pub menu is available Sunday through Wednesday from 3:30 P.M. to 11 P.M. and Thursday through Sunday from 3:30 P.M. to 12 midnight.

Tours: Available from 11:30 A.M. until closing time. Also specially arranged in conjunction with Old Town Trolley (see page 106).

Gift Shop: No, but retail goods are sold.

Parking: Nearby, at Holyoke Street Parking Garage

T-stop: Red Line at Harvard Square

"Honest Food, Real Beer" is not only the slogan for John Harvard's Brew House, it's the company's mission statement. Voted "Best Brewpub" for the second year in a row by *Boston Magazine* in the annual "Best of Boston" poll, John Harvard's continues to remain a favorite of pub-goers looking for a place where, in the words of the magazine's editors, ". . . the beers both complement and counterpoint the American country-fare cuisine, to the satisfaction of discriminating drinkers and diners."

Internet friend Kit Wilcox loves the blackened catfish sandwich, which is served with lettuce, tomato, red onion, and house-made tartar sauce on a Kaiser roll, accompanied by a creamy cucumber salad. On the day I visited for lunch, the warm salad of grilled lamb and house-made, fresh-herb sausage with couscous, scallions, tomatoes, black olives, feta cheese, and Lola Rosa lettuce was incredible. The service was excellent, and even though I ate alone at the bar, I was made to feel very welcome by the bartender and manager, who personally served all lunch patrons ordering food from the bar area that day.

The Beer: Director of brewery operations Tim Morse keeps the John Harvard staff busy, not only with making the beer, but with learning what characteristics make a bad beer bad. Morse has developed a program where he tastes and tests beers other than his own, brought directly from store shelves to his brewery, to detect problems that often occur after a beer is bottled or during fermentation. He also "spikes" some of the beers to make the defect more pronounced. In turn, his brewers can educate the other staff to recognize these qualities.

In a recent *Providence Journal-Bulletin* article entitled, "When Bad Things Happen to Good Beer," writer Donald Breed sat in on one of these sessions and observed that among other glitches, oxidation can make a beer stale. Telltale flavors are "bready, cardboardy or papery, and can happen when beer was bottled with excessive amounts of air—more than .7 milliliters of air per 12-ounce container."

Problems can also occur because of incomplete fermentation. Acetaldehyde causes grassy, green-apple, and sherry flavors, and Breed notes that diacetyl results in what is described as a buttery flavor. That's a quality desirable in some wines but not in beer, especially in the sample that brewer Morse had spiked; it was reminiscent of the fake butter on theater popcorn.

The Food: Chef Joe Kubik leads the culinary effort at John Harvard's, as well as the Union Station Brewery in Providence, Rhode Island, and his skill has been collecting raves since JH opened in 1992. Specialties of the house include "starters" that are priced from $3.95 to $5.95 and range from pub fare (like wings, nachos, and potato skins) to mushroom fritters with Parmesan and cracked-black-pepper dip; grilled house-made-sausage skewers with two mustards; and house-made mozzarella and vine-ripened tomatoes. Special salads (besides the grilled lamb) are grilled fresh tuna-steak with crushed peppercorns, served over an assortment of field greens, warm roasted potatoes, little vegetables, tomatoes, and artichokes; and fresh Atlantic salmon and orzo pasta with yellow patty pan squash, asparagus, tomatoes, basil, and greens.

Master brewer Tim Morse (left) and executive chef Joe Kubik team up for the John Harvard's Brew House annual Summer Beer and Barbecue Festival.

Burgers, grilled pizzas, and pasta dishes round out these classic pub entrées: award-winning chili— "Slow-Cooked Chunky Beef and Bean Chili," to be exact—which won the *Boston Magazine* Firehouse Chili Cookoff and is served with cheddar cheese, fresh tomatoes, sour cream, and a grilled flour tortilla; old-fashioned chicken pot pie; grilled meatloaf with mashed potatoes, green beans, gravy, and battered onion rings; and a mixed grill including house-made chorizo, andouille, and peppered-garlic sausage, served with fresh herbs over mashed potatoes and wild-mushroom/cabbage ragout. From the smokehouse, savor either an apple-smoked half chicken, marinated and slow smoked, or a rack of hickory-smoked baby back ribs. Entrée prices run from $8.95 to $12.95.

Each month, head brewer Brian Sanford and executive chef Frank L'Heureux present a "Brewery Dinner," featuring kitchen masterpieces matched with John Harvard's beers and ales. Reservations are required, and the price (in 1996) was $39.95 per person, which included tax and gratuity. Each evening begins with hors d'oeuvres served, for example, with All American Light Lager, then proceeds into several courses from there. The February 1996 menu consisted of bruschetta of house-made mozzarella with roasted peppers, creamy hummus and tapenade; Maine lobster cocktail with fennel/parsley salad, served with John Harvard's Pale

Ale; roasted monkfish and sautéed spinach with smoky tomato/caper butter sauce laced with Extra Special Bitter and served with more of the same; "Intermezzo Sorbet" of barley malt, Ceylon tea, and Amber Ale; venison stew with vegetables, mashed potatoes and stout gravy served with Big Bad Bock; and, for dessert, toasted orange pound cake with black currant raisins, blood oranges, and malted whipped cream enjoyed with Pilgrims' Porter.

John Harvard's Brew House

One Worcester Road, (at the Shopper's World Mall);
Framingham, MA 01701; 508-775-BEER (2337)

Hours: Monday through Wednesday from 11:30 A.M. to 1 A.M.; Thursday through Saturday from 11:30 A.M. to 2 A.M.; and Sunday from 11:30 A.M. to 11 P.M.

John Harvard's second Massachusetts location opened amid much fanfare in September 1996, claiming to be the first MetroWest brewpub to offer both top-fermented ales and bottom-fermented lagers under one roof. This "first" in suburban brewing is overseen by Brian Sanford, former head brewer at the first JH pub, and beer selections include John Harvard's Pale Ale, Old Willy IPA, Nut Brown Ale, and Pilgrim's Porter. The lager is All American Light Lager. Rotating seasonal selections will also be available.

Hugo Benjumea, former sous chef at the Harvard Square location, heads up the kitchen in Framingham, offering a menu highlighted by baked, grilled, smoked, and barbecued specialties. Don't miss the weekend "Brewer's Brunch" menu and monthly "Brewery Dinners," which feature a special five-course menu pairing beer and food for a fixed price, much like the events at the Harvard Square facility.

Main Street Brewing Company

244 Main Street; Worcester, MA 01608; 508-753-6700; 800-621-BREW

Lots of money went into this place, but the most recent word (in late '96) was that the company was struggling to stay alive. Call ahead, and if the Main Street folks are there, pay them a visit and give them your support.

Mass Bay Brewing Company
306 Northern Avenue; Boston, MA 02210; 617-574-9551

Tours: Friday and Saturday at 1 P.M.

Gift Shop: Yes. Harpoon brew wear is also available by direct mail. Call for a catalog.

The makers of Harpoon beers claim that Mass Bay Brewing Company (founded in 1987) is the largest brewery in Massachusetts. They also appear to have the brew-

Checking out some new equipment.

ery tour down to an art. Held in the "Tap Room," which overlooks the 5,000-square-foot brewery below, tours are the responsibility of the entire staff. Depending on the date of your visit, you may find the president, Richard Doyle, guiding you through the Harpoon brewing process.

After the tour, you can sample the many Harpoon products and peruse the huge beer bottle and can collection, while brewing operations take place in full view. If you can't make the weekend tours, and you work in the city, come for the "5:30 Club" tours. This is a great way for the office crew to relax after work on Tuesdays, Wednesdays, and Thursdays. Your group must number at least fifteen people but no more than eighty; you have to make reservations in advance; and you must send in a refundable deposit of $1.00 per person before your scheduled evening.

The Beer: Harpoon beers and ales can be found now in more than four-

teen states along the East Coast, as far south as the Tampa, Florida, area. The company's regular lineup includes its flagship beer, Harpoon Ale, as well as Harpoon Light, Harpoon IPA, and Harpoon Pilsner. Seasonals, which debut amidst much hoopla, are Harpoon Stout, ushered in at a huge St. Patrick's Day benefit bash; Harpoon

Alt, which is celebrated at a mid-June birthday party called "Brewstock"; Harpoon Octoberfest, poured in the first week of October to the music of a live oomp-pah band; and Harpoon Winter Warmer, enjoyed at a party held to express thanks to all the brewery's friends and fans (proceeds go to local charities helping the less

fortunate at Christmas). These events have hosted more than 10,000 people at once!

The happy Harpooners like to keep in touch with their customers and will be glad to put you on the mailing list for their quarterly newsletter to keep you up to date on their doings and brewings. Call the brewery number, wade through their voicemail, and ask to get on the list!

Middlesex Brewing Company

844 Woburn Street; Wilmington, MA 01887; 508-657-8100

Tours: By appointment

Owner/brewer Brian Friguliette has made a quantum leap from the two-barrel brewing system he used in his Burlington home to the twenty-five-barrel system in the new Wilmington facility. His beers are available on draught and in twelve-ounce bottles throughout Massachusetts, and he has plans to expand elsewhere in New England. Friguliette currently produces Middlesex Raspberry Wheat, Middlesex Brown Ale, and Middlesex Oatmeal Stout. These offerings are featured at Redbone's in Somerville and The Sunset Grille in Allston.

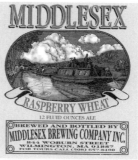

Mill City Brewing Company

199 Cabot Street; Lowell, MA 01852; 508-937-1200

Tours: Call ahead for times.

LBC has undergone extensive changes since its original incarnation and now offers a new product line of appropriately-named brews celebrating Lowell's fame as the former textile capital of the world. Boarding House Pale Ale, Spindle Porter, and Chocolate Raspberry Wheat are some of the beers available in twelve- and twenty-two-ounce bottles, and on draught.

Area Attractions:

• **Lowell National Historical Park**

246 Market Street; Lowell, MA 01852; 508-970-5000

Walk through this restored mill building and learn about life as a mill girl in the mid-1800s. There are exhibits on immigrants, water power, and labor history. Guided walking tours are available, and—in summer—there are barge and trolley tours.

• **Tsongas Industrial History Center**

Boott Cotton Mills Museum; 400 Foot of John Street;
Lowell, MA 01852; 508-970-5080

There are lots of hands-on activities at this former cotton mill.

• **American Textile Museum**

491 Dutton Street; Lowell, MA 01852; 508-441-0400

Textiles, tools, machinery, and images tell the story of cloth-making in the United States, highlighted by a working woolen mill and weave room.

• **New England Quilt Museum**

18 Shattuck Street; Lowell, MA 01852; 508-452-4207

National and international exhibits display the finest quilts in the world.

• **Whistler House Museum of Art**

243 Worthen Street; Lowell, MA 01852; 508-452-7641

This is the birthplace of Whistler's Mother's son (James Abbott McNeill Whistler, if you didn't guess).

The Modern Brewer

152 Commonwealth Avenue; West Concord, MA 01752; 617-498-0400

Tours: Call ahead.

Originally a home-brew supply store, The Modern Brewer has decided to make the leap to brewing its own beers. Fat Cat ESB, Big Shoes Ale, and Modern Brewer IPA will lead the lineup to begin with. You can sample them at more than two dozen restaurants and pubs in Massachusetts, including Redbone's in Somerville, Cornwall's in Boston, and New Mother of India in Waltham.

North East Brewing Company

1314 Commonwealth Avenue; Boston, MA (Allston) 02215; 617-566-6699

Located in the former Play it Again, Sam building, NEBC is headed up by Dann Paquette, who will be brewing in a fifteen-barrel PUB system. Bostonia Blonde, Black Sow Stout, Triple Black Wheat Ale, and MacFearsome Scotch Ale are some of the beers Paquette will be serving.

Northampton Brewery

11 Brewster Court; Northampton, MA 01060; 413-584-9903

Located in the heart of town, Northampton Brewery occupies the former carriage house of the Brewster Estate. Owner Janet Egleston, with brother Peter, can be considered the brewster in this three-micro family. Northampton started it all off in 1987, and now siblings have opened The Portsmouth Brewery (page 38) and Smuttynose Brewery (page 41), both in New Hampshire.

The Beer: Using a ten-barrel, J.B. Northwest system, head brewer Chris O'Connor turns out more than a dozen beers, including seasonals and specialties. When I took the tour last October, NHB featured the following: Byzantine Blonde; Alternator, Northhampton's version of a traditional Alt-style ale; a highly hopped, unfiltered Pale Ale; the brewery's most popular beer, Amber Lager; Golden Lager; Old Brown Dog, winner of the silver medal at the 1989 Great American Beer Festival; Daniel Shays Best Bitter; and Hoover's Porter. Specialties include Weizenheimer, a summer favorite; Black Cat Stout; Pumpkin Ale; Spring Bock; Octoberfest; Steamer, made in a single batch only for St. Patrick's Day; and an annual Holiday Special made around Christmas time.

The Food: The menu is regularly updated and varied, but count on pub fare, as well as special sandwiches, pizzas, and spicy selections such as "Tiger Chicken," chili, grilled chicken with jerk seasoning, spicy shell-on shrimp, and an appetizer called "Cheese and Ale Spread." Made with three cheeses, NHB's Amber Ale, and spices, it's served with crackers and raw vegetables. A children's menu is available at both lunch and dinner.

Old Harbor Brewing Company

577 Main Street (The Cablevision Building); Hudson, MA 01749;
508-562-6992

E-mail: OHBC@tiac.com

Internet access: http://www.webmart.com/Pilgrim.html

Tours: Saturdays at 1 P.M. and 3 P.M.

"Beer is living proof that God loves us and wants to see us happy" quipped Ben Franklin back in the old old days, and this pearl of wisdom still serves quite nicely as Old Harbor's philosophy—so much so that it adorns the company's stationary. Built in only ninety days, probably an industry record, Old Harbor Brewing Company is located in central Massachusetts, fifteen minutes from Worcester.

Old Harbor Brewing Company's owners originally produced their beers at Ipswich Brewing Company but decided to build their own facility after perfecting their recipes. Setting up in December 1994, they began brewing in March 1995 and are now expanding their capacity to 3,800 barrels (from the original 1,200). They have more than 325 accounts, most of which hold regular "brewery dinners" that match Old Harbor Brewing Company brews with multi-course meals.

The crew also stays visible in the community by sponsoring several benefit events a year, including a five-kilometer road race on Thanksgiving Day for the National Multiple Sclerosis Society. Participants "run" away with a T-shirt, pint glass, and sixty-four-ounce growler of beer to enjoy with their turkey dinners. The Old Harbor Brewing Company brewers also welcome volunteers, affectionately called "brewpies" (as in "groupies"), to work at their facility. And if it's too early in the day for a beer, they sell their own blend of coffee called Morning Brew.

The Beer: Bold moves are common at Old Harbor Brewing Company. Co-owner Ed Yost is even spearheading an effort to rejuvenate the region's hop-growing industry by setting an example at the brewery site: The members of his crew are planting and cultivating their own Cascade, Perle, and Eroica hops,

which are harvested every October and used to brew Pilgrim Harvest IPA. In 1995, they produced more than 100 barrels (3,100 gallons) of their hoppy brew, described as having a medium body, a light-amber to orange color, a mild maltiness and floral hop aroma, and a toasted-malt, citrus, and herbal-hoppy flavor. The company's Pilgrim Nut Brown Ale won the "Best of Boston" award in 1994.

Area Attractions:

• **Fall Foliage**

Generally, the color in central Massachusetts foliage peaks between October 5 and October 18. For the best routes, call the foliage hotline at 800-227-MASS.

• **Apple Picking**

Minutes away from Hudson is "apple country." In Stow, Bolton, and Harvard, which are clustered together, you can drink fresh cider, buy Halloween pumpkins, and help the kids gather the apples you'll use to make your holiday pies. Call the town offices or the Massachusetts Department of Tourism at 617-727-6525 for more information.

• **Nashoba Valley Winery**
  100 Wattaquottoc Hill Road; Bolton, MA 01740; 508-779-5521
  Tours: Saturday and Sunday
  My former employer, Jack Partridge, makes award-winning fruit wines at Nashoba, which is set on rolling farmland where he grows apples for one of the company's wines. Head over for a tour and some tasting.

Old Town Trolley

329 W. Second Street; South Boston, MA 02127; 617-269-7150

Tours: By reservation only. Proper identification is required of all passengers. The fee of $38.00 includes transportation, food, beer, tax, and gratuities.

For a memorable three-hour tour beer lovers have to try Old Town Trolley's brewpub excursion, the first one of its kind in the country. For $38.00 you will be treated to a ride around Boston and Cambridge in a cozy, authentically styled, all-weather trolley. Beginning at John Harvard's Brew House in Harvard Square, you will have chef L'Heureux's appetizers and sip two of the house beers, then its on to Commonwealth Brewing Company near the Fleet Center. Chef Glenn Jordan will offer you two types of Commonwealth beer, which will complement "The Best Damn Yankee Ribs in America." The final stop is brew moon, where one of chef Don Chappelle's desserts will be served with brewer Tony Vieira's handcrafted beers.

Between stops, a guide will deliver intriguing narrative about Boston's microbrewing history, and inside at least one of the pubs, you'll be given a tour of the brewery. The Trolley holds forty-one passengers and is perfect for special groups and parties. If you have only one afternoon in the Boston/Cambridge area, do this tour!

Olde Cape Cod Beverage Company

P.O. Box 778; South Dennis, MA 02563;
508-385-3954

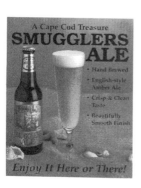

A Cape Cod Treasure
SMUGGLERS ALE
• Hand Brewed
• English-style Amber Ale
• Crisp & Clean Taste
• Beautifully Smooth Finish

Enjoy It Here or There!

Owner John Mincieli contract-brews his Smugglers Ale, which he proudly describes as an amber, lighter in flavor than traditional English ales. Served throughout the Cape and available in liquor stores in twelve-ounce bottles, Smugglers Ale deserves a taste if you're traveling that way.

Olde Salem Brewery and Grille

278 Derby Street; Salem, MA 01970; 508-777-2260

Like brew moon's Tony Vieira, Gregg Norris is a graduate of the Anheuser-Busch pilot brewery in St. Louis. The first brewpub in "Witch City" is within walking distance of the historical attractions in Salem.

The Beer: Norris offers Scarlet Letter Red, Golden Ale, Hawthorne Honey Ale, and Midnight Stout, all brewed in a fifteen-barrel PUB Brewing system. There are also seasonals like last year's Old Man Winter Yuletide Ale.

Area Attractions:

• **Salem Witch Museum**

Washington Square; Salem, MA 01970; 508-744-1692

Starting with its phone number's last four digits, which match the year the Salem witch trials took place, the museum has fun with the bizarre events that put the town on the map. Its recent advertising campaign declares, "Experience Mass. hysteria" and "We're wicked good." Live presentations reenact the 1692 trials: "the innocent victims come alive and plead to a deaf justice system."

Owen O'Leary's Brewpub

319 Speen Street; Natick, MA 01760; 508-650-0972

Blair Potts has headed up the brewing effort at O'Leary's, which is located right off the Massachusetts Turnpike in the Hampton Inn. He is training Dan Climo to take over making Owen O'Leary's Light, Irish red ale, stout, brown ale, cherry stout, and honey blackberry ale. Selections change frequently. The menu features nightly specials like Mix and Match Mania. For $9.95, you can select portions of mussels, prime rib, baked haddock, and many other dishes to make up your own entrée. On other nights you can get a complete dinner for $7.95. Try matching that anywhere else in the greater Boston area, especially with a place that makes its own beer.

Paper City Brewing Company
108 Cabot Street; Holyoke, MA 01040; 413-535-1588

Tours: Call ahead for times

Paper City was opened by Jay Hebert in November 1994, and brewer Rick Quackenbush is producing the company's beer on a twenty-barrel Brew House system. Located in Holyoke, once one of the largest producers of fine paper and stationary products, the brewery occupies the fifth floor of an old textile mill in the downtown area.

The Beer: Dam Ale, named for a river dam nearby, is the current brew. Future beers will be a lager and some seasonals. Bottling is targeted for late 1997.

Peabody Brewing Company
26 Walnut Street; Peabody, MA 01960; 508-538-9995

Mark Manning, a former airplane mechanic, and his brother Michael, a geologist, turned their love for home-brewing into a full-blown micro. Just licensed in January 1997, the Manning brothers have turned out Nor'easter Pale Ale, the favorite of friends and family who encouraged the pair to brew for a living. You can also try their product at the Century House on Route 114 in Peabody.

The People's Pint
24 Federal Street; Greenfield, MA 01301; 413-773-0333

Opened January 1, 1997, The People's Pint's brewing effort is headed by Dan Young, formerly of the Windham Brewery in Burlington, Vermont. Young is serving happy Greenfielders Brake Shoe Porter, Provider Pale

Ale, Broad Fork Stout, and Extra Ordinary Ale, all made with organically grown Australian hops. Seasonals will round out the list. Emphasizing pub fare, the People's Pint also serves pizza, burritos, and some Mediterranean dishes, as well as homemade breads and desserts. Dan Young's ginger ale is also available. Sunday evenings bring Irish folk music.

Pioneer Valley Brewpub

51–59 Taylor Street; Springfield, MA 01103; 413-732-2739

Prevented from brewing on the premises by a city bylaw, the folks at Pioneer have their beers made by other microbreweries in New England. The menu ranges from fine dining to casual.

Salem Beer Works

278 Derby Street; Salem, MA 01970; 508-874-9965

This sister to brewpub Boston Beer Works opened in May 1996. Brewing operations at both places are supervised by Steve Slesar, but Salem has its own brews. Salem Pale Ale, Witch City Red, Black Bat Stout, Pumpkin Head Ale, and North Shore Light accompany the menu, which features brick-oven-baked pizza. The remainder of the cuisine is the same as that at the Boston location.

Underground Brewery

518 Lincoln Street; Marlborough, MA 01752; 508-874-9965

Scott Ludke is in the enviable position of being busy, growing 10 to 15 percent per month. Unfortunately, that means he can't give tours of his facility now. Console yourself by trying his beer at the No Name Restaurant in Boston, the Wildwood Restaurant in Marlborough, or the Mountain Barn in Westminster. Or, buy Underground Premium Ale (a red ale), Dirty Blonde, and Old Sudbury Ale at Kappy's Liquors (Sudbury or Peabody), Marty's Liquors (Allston or Newton), and DeLuca's (on Newbury Street, Boston). Ludke also makes beer for restaurants that wish to bottle their own private label. Lucky participants are the Wayside Inn (Sudbury), Houlihan's, The Castle (Leicester) and the Holiday Inn Plaza Hotel (Worcester).

Wachusett Brewing Company

175 State Road East, Route 2A; P.O. Box 417; Westminster, MA 01473; 508-874-9965

Tours: Saturdays at 1 P.M. and 3 P.M.

Gift shop: Open 9 A.M. to 6 P.M., it offers ales in growlers, shirts, glasses, and more.

E-mail: wachuset@tiac.net

The president and co-owner of Wachusett Brewing Company, twenty-six-year-old Ned LaFortune III, has a clear vision of what his company is and where it's going. He and his partners, head brewer Peter Quinn, and plant engineer Kevin Buckler, were classmates at nearby Worcester Polytechnic Institute, all studying for careers in various technical fields. While working as a project engineer for an architect firm, LaFortune began home-brewing and planning his own brewery. When they were ready to take the plunge, the three partners quit their jobs, hit up friends and family for capital, and launched Wachusett Brewing Company.

Less than four months after their opening, the trio had to quadruple their output to keep up with customer demand, and they are already being approached by Boston-area restaurants and bars that want to carry their ales. LaFortune, however, insists that WBC has no intention of expanding beyond Massachusetts.

Internet friend Peter Weimeyer raved about Wachusett's tour ("all three guys spent an hour with me as we sampled the ales and talked brew") and praised their ales ("all are fresh, hoppy, and distinctive").

(Left to right) Head brewer Peter Quinn, president Ned La Fortune III, plant engineer Kevin Buckler, and Molson, Ned's retriever.

To reach Wachusett from the east, take Route 2 to Exit 27; follow Depot Road a half-mile, turn right onto Route 2A through the railroad underpass, and stop at Westminster Place. The brewery is in the rear of the building. If you're approaching from the west, take Route 2 to Exit 29 (Routes 140 and 2A); turn right, and follow 2A east for 1½ miles. WBC is on the right, just beyond the railroad underpass.

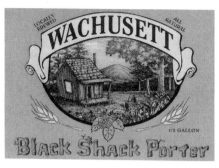

The Beer: Country Ale, Wachusett's flagship beer, is a light-colored, medium-bodied pale ale with a complex hop balance and slightly sweet, malty finish; Country Nut Brown Ale is smooth, full-bodied, and dark-brown in color, with a rich, malty finish; Wachusett IPA is a light-colored, medium-bodied ale with aggressive hop character. LaFortune and his partners also produce several seasonals, including Black Shack Porter (February through May), a big, flavorable beer, black as midnight, with a thick brown head; Wild Berry Wheat Ale (May through September); Octoberfest Ale (September through November); and Special Christmas Ale (November through January).

Area Attractions:

- **Fall Foliage**

  The color peaks between October 3 and 16.

- **Wachusett Ski Area**

  Mountain Road; Princeton, MA 01541; 1-800-SKI-1234

  The ski area offers a "skycar" ride for foliage viewers in the fall and serves WBC ales in its restaurant.

- **Red Apple Farm**

  Phillipston, MA 01331

  Come and pick your own apples!

Watch City Brewing Company

256 Moody Street; Waltham, MA 02154; 617-647-4000

The first restaurant/brewery to open in the hometown of the famous Waltham Watch Company, newcomer Watch City Brewing Company opened amid much local fanfare on the last weekend of March in 1996. General manager Frank McLaughlin sounded exhausted when I called for information

on the Monday after a debut that he called "very busy."

Owner Jocelyn Fryer comments, "My husband Jonathan and I lived for a time in England, so after college and law school there seemed nothing left to do but open a brewpub."

Featuring its signature chowder and other upscale dishes, the 180-seat restaurant provides greater-Boston residents with a place to enjoy hand-crafted beers without braving Boston traffic, although I often call Route 128, along which Waltham lies, the "Hail Mary Highway" for the crazy driving that takes place there.

The Beer: Tick Tock Ale is a golden and light-bodied brew that has only a touch of hops. Orient Ale is similar to an English Bitter in that it features balanced maltiness, a deep hop character from imported English hops and moderate bitterness. Titan Ale is a big-bodied showcase for the Northwest's finest hops, while Moody Street Stout is a dark and unfiltered brew that's served with a creamy head and has hints of coffee and chocolate.

The Food: Appetizers include the house specialty, Bermuda fish chowder served with Outerbridge sherry peppers and Gosling Black Rum; crispy calamari tossed with balsamic vinegar and pepperoncini; and pan-seared crab cakes with ginger/soy vinaigrette. Salads go beyond Caesar with chicken, which Watch City offers, to grilled-shrimp salad with cilantro and sun-dried tomato vinaigrette; Mediterranean seared-tuna salad with lemon/herb vinai-grette; and spinach salad with seared scallops and a warm pancetta dressing.

COURTESY OF WATCH CITY BREWING COMPANY

Entrées include sandwiches and burgers; a German-sausage sampler with sauerkraut and mashed potatoes; seared salmon, seasoned with mustard seeds and served with grilled veggies and a Dijon hollandaise; grilled tuna with orange-butter sauce

General manager Frank McLaughlin with owners Jocelyn and Jonathan Fryer.

and "shoepeg" corn flan; and a couple of pasta dishes.

Jocelyn Fryer happily shares her chef's recipe for beer-battered fish:

Watch City Brewing Company's Beer Batter Cod

(Batter recipe makes enough to dredge twenty-four servings; reduce proportions as appropriate for your use.)

    1 pitcher Orient Ale (an ESB or other bitter can substitute)
    1 can Coco Lopez
    1 stem fresh cilantro, chopped (or 1 tablespoon dried)
    1 tablespoon Old Bay seasoning
    1 tablespoon dry mustard
    1 tablespoon black pepper
    2 quarts flour
    10 eggs

Combine all ingredients. Dredge seven-ounce cod fillets in the batter, and deep fry in 375° oil until crispy and golden brown.

Area Attractions:

• Charles River Museum of Industry
    154 Moody Street; Waltham, MA 02154; 617-893-5410
    This museum acknowledges the city of Waltham's contribution to the

Industrial Revolution and features The Textile Mill, the first modern factory in the world; the Waltham Watch Company, where modern machinery turned out the first factory-made watches; and the Metz auto plant. Along with the other car manufacturers set up along the Charles River — Orient, Stanley Steamer, and Ford — Metz helped perfect the moving-assembly-line system.

RHODE ISLAND

In Rhode Island there is an area where several microbreweries/brewpubs are in relatively close proximity. This grouping is given below, along with a consolidated list of area attractions that are also worth a visit.

PROVIDENCE AREA

Trinity Brewhouse (see page 117)
Union Station Brewery (see page 117)

AREA ATTRACTIONS

Providence is a good walking city. Close by Union Station Brewery is The Arcade, the oldest indoor shopping center in the United States. Built in 1828 and now on the National Register of Historic Places, The Arcade contains an eclectic collection of shops featuring international products.

- **Museum of Art/Rhode Island School of Design**
  224 Benefit Street; Providence, RI 02906; 401-465-6500
  The museum houses classical art from Greece and Rome, as well as American and European painting and sculpture from the Middle Ages to the present, among other exhibitions. Kids will love to learn that leading children's-book author Chris Van Allsburg (*Jumanji, The Wretched Stone, The Polar Express*) teaches at RISD, the school's local nickname (pronounced "riz-dee"). Call to see if any of his illustrations are on display.
- **Johnson and Wales Culinary Archives and Museum**
  315 Harborside Boulevard; Providence, RI 02905; 401-455-2805
  Containing more than 200,000 culinary items dating from 3,000 B.C. to the present, this is a cook's paradise.

Coddington Brewing Company

210 Coddington Highway; Middletown, RI 02842; 401-847-6690

Just when I despaired of ever finding any information about this brew-pub, I received e-mail from Internet friend Kevin Koziol. He and his wife have enjoyed dining at Coddington many times, and he reports their favorites: In the beer category, the Pumpkin Ale and Hazelnut Porter garner raves. For food, Kevin orders the boneless buffalo wings every time he goes, and he has tried the mozzarella sticks and onion rings, finding both good. Several pasta, salad, pizza, sandwich, and pub selections round out the offerings, and there is a kids' menu, too.

Emerald Isle Brew Works

Street address: 1454 Main Street; West Warwick, RI 02893
Mailing address: 11 Bank Street; West Warwick, RI 02893
401-828-2537 (brewery); 401-821-3149 (office)

Tours: Call brewery for times

Ray McConnell took time out from his busy dental practice to talk about his new business, Emerald Isle. Ray began home-brewing in 1987 and now serves as his firm's head brewer, with son Michael assisting. Using authentic "beer engines" crafted in Derbyshire, England, McConnell's crew  draws Emerald Isle beers from a cellar-temperature cask right to glasses at the bar. These brews have not been filtered or artificially carbonated, and Ray states, "all the B-vitamins are there, like liquid bread."

Trinity Brewhouse
186 Fountain Street; Providence, RI 02903; 401-453-2337

Union Station Brewery
36 Exchange Street; Providence, RI 02903; 401-274-2739

Tours: On request

Gift shop: Retail merchandise is available

The first microbrewery to open in Rhode Island since Narragansett closed its doors in 1982, Union Station has iced its place in our littlest state's micro stature. Awards have abounded: *Rhode Island Monthly* magazine has handed it "Best Place to go for a Beer,"
"Best Singles Joint," "Best Wings," and "Best Chili. And, the locals gave Union Station the "Peoples Choice Award" at the area's pasta festival.

The Beer: Norm Allaire heads up the brewing effort at Union Station, which merged with the owners of John Harvard's Brew House (page 96). He offers Providence City Pale Ale, Golden Spike Ale, East Coast Common Beer, and seasonals Winter Stout and Winter Lager. These beers are available only at USB, so if you're traveling north to Boston, belly up at this charming renovated train station and enjoy lunch or dinner and brews.

The Food: Chef Joe Protano and staff serve up extraordinary pizzas, whose crusts are made with spent grains from the brewing process. "The malted grain renders a rich flavorful crust," according to Protano. *Rhode Island Monthly* voted Union Station's offering "Best Pizza Appetizer." Varieties include Pizza One: mozzarella, basil, Parmesan, garlic, and chunky tomato sauce; Pizza Two: house-made sausage, roasted peppers, tomatoes, pesto, and provolone; Pizza Three: Gulf shrimp, yellow and red tomatoes, pesto, and provolone; and Pizza Four: spinach, broccoli, garlic, sun-dried tomatoes, pesto, mozzarella and fontina cheeses. All are $7.95.

Appetizers are appealing. Enjoy a sampling of bruschetta; chili; pan-seared spicy chicken wings; mussels steamed in Golden Spike Ale; roasted and grilled Portobello mushrooms, served over spinach salad with goat cheese and roasted peppers; warm leek tart and house-made, maple-smoked salmon; and ale-battered onion rings.

The lunch menu features a large assortment of sandwiches and salads, including a knife-and-fork steak sandwich with herbed new potatoes, caramelized onions, and garlic bread; a Reuben; and a grilled, pesto-marinated chicken breast on focaccia with house-made mayonnaise, mozzarella, roasted peppers, lettuce, tomato, and artichoke.

The list of dinner entrées makes choosing even harder: the "Best Pasta" winner is chicken with penne, tossed with house-made tasso ham, mushrooms, peas, and garlic in a white-wine/cream sauce. Then there are a duet of smoked-mozzarella and roasted-garlic/spinach raviolis with fresh tomato/basil sauce and a warm arugula salad, roasted red peppers, eggplant, and black olives; spicy grilled catfish over black beans with mango salsa, flour tortillas, and sour cream; the Union Station brewery plate featuring chorizo, andouille, and fresh-herb sausages — hand-ground, smoked daily, grilled, and served with scalloped-potato pie and braised cabbage; an ale-marinated flank steak with "red bliss" mashed potatoes, oven-dried tomatoes, and grilled vegetables; and a house rack of hickory-smoked baby back pork ribs—dry-rubbed, slow smoked, and served with baked beans, scalloped potatoes, and coleslaw. Most dinner entrées fall in the $9.95 range; lunches average $6.95. There is a special menu for Sunday brunch.

Once considered as the New England city least likely to provide a vacation stop, Providence has been revitalized over the past two decades, and Union Station is in the heart of it at "WaterPlace." Located in one of five refurbished buildings behind the State House, USB occupies the space that formerly was the city's main train station. Remnants of that incarnation are visible in the brewery, which also displays much Narragansett brewery memorabilia.

CONNECTICUT

Connecticut has one area where several microbreweries/brewpubs are in relatively close proximity. This grouping is given below, along with a consolidated list of area attractions that are also worth a visit.

Connecticut is a little behind northern New England in the number of brewpubs and micros open, but it won't be long before the Nutmeg State catches up, since the income level of its population can support dozens of niche beer establishments. Many thanks are due to Internet correspondent Simon Wesley, a doctoral candidate in physics who is also a dedicated pub "crawler" and home-brewer. Simon braved the winter weather to travel to several of these pubs, gather menus, and take photos for me.

NEW HAVEN AREA

The Bru Room at BAR (see page 123)
New Haven Brewing Company/The Brewery Restaurant (see page 126)
Nutmeg Brewery (see page 128)

AREA ATTRACTIONS

You can't help but get a good dose of culture visiting the home of Yale University.

- **Yale University Art Gallery**
  1111 Chapel Street at York Street; New Haven, CT 06520; 203-432-0600
  Since 1832, the museum's collection has grown to more than 100,000 objects, dating from ancient Egypt to the present and including paintings by van Gogh, Manet, Monet, and Picasso.

- **Yale Repertory Theatre**
  Corner of Chapel and York Streets; New Haven, CT 06520; 203-432-1234
  Performances are staged from October through May.

- **Pardee Rose Gardens**
  180 Park Avenue; New Haven, CT 06515; 203-946-8025
  Catch more than fifty varieties of roses in bloom from April through October, peaking during June and July.

Alewife Grille and Brewery

2935 Main Street; Glastonbury, CT 06033; 860-659-8686

Tours: Thursday and Friday from noon to 4 P.M.; call for weekend times.

Gift shop: Call for hours.

Tom O'Neill, who is both an attorney and a CPA, began home-brewing with wife Jennifer in 1989. After the bug "bit," they began investigating opening a brewpub. As Jennifer claims, "The April '96 opening of the Alewife Grille was the culmination of years of research and planning."

The Beer: The O'Neills named two of their beers after their daughters —Miss Elizabeth's Porter and Sweet Caroline's Irish Red Ale. Other brews on the menu are Cellarmaster ESB, Bombay Express IPA, and some of Shipyard Brewing Company's recipes, which are brewed under license, on the premises.

Area Attractions:

- **Connecticut's Audubon Center at Glastonbury**

  1361 Main Street; Glastonbury, CT 06033; 203-860-8402

  View exhibits on native flora and fauna of the Connecticut River eco-system. Adjacent to forty-eight-acre Earle Park and its trail system, the Center offers year-round programs.

(Left to right) chef Adam Greaves, brewer J. J. Ranas, and co-owner Tom O'Neill.

Bank Street Brewing Company

65 Bank Street; Stamford, CT 06903; 203-325-2739

Brewer Ted Steen makes six of his own brews, as well as Shipyard Export Ale and Goat Island Light. As a licensed "Pugsley's Pub," Bank Street keeps freshly made Shipyard products flowing in the Nutmeg State.

The Brewhouse Restaurant at New England Brewing Company

13 Marshall Street; South Norwalk, CT 06854; 203-853-9110

Tours: Wednesday, Saturday, and Sunday from 11 A.M. to 4 P.M.; groups are limited to thirty people.

Lush is the only word to describe the recent expansion of NEBC's micro business to include a brewery/restaurant. The huge, copper mash kettle

dominates the brewery floor and is surrounded by dining tables. *Bon Appetit* magazine selected the company's Gold Stock Ale as one of the top ten microbrewed beers for 1994.

The Beer: New England's other brews include: Atlantic Amber, a gold-medal winner in the Altbier category at the Great American Beer Festival in 1993; Light Lager, which took the bronze medal at the 1995 World Beer Championships; American Wheat; Oatmeal Stout; and Golden Night.

The Food: Chef executed and highly original, the Brewhouse's menu can be considered on the high end of the scale: both the price and gourmet quality of the selections distinguish them from casual brewpub fare. Appetizers include oysters and clams on the

New England Brewing Company makes the beer for The Brewhouse.

half-shell; smoked Maine salmon; seafood sausage; mussels steamed in wheat beer; and game sausage with sweet-potato salad. Sandwiches pique the interest and appetite, beg-

ging to be accompanied by beer. Try the roast loin of pork, with spicy cabbage, romaine, and cucumbers; the smoked salmon, with red onion, lettuce, tomato, and fresh tartar sauce; and the Brewhouse burger, with smoked bacon and cheddar cheese.

Entrées run from $12.95 for marinated roast duck to $29.95 for the daily beer dinner, where three courses are matched with the Brewhouse's beer. Particularly interesting are roast Maine cod with a stout-and-red-wine sauce; braised lamb shanks with barley and stout; sauerbraten marinated in oatmeal stout and served with spaetzle; and smoked bratwurst served with beer-braised cabbage and sweet potatoes.

The Brewhouse decor deserves extra mention. Owners Marcia and Dick King spent a couple of million dollars renovating the single-story warehouse in historic South Norwalk, adding a full basement, second story, and clock tower. The beer-brewing process is broken down into steps and described by plaques placed around the restaurant. There is also an extensive collection of beer trays, signs, bottles, and other memorabilia from many of the more than twenty breweries that existed in Connecticut before Prohibition. The wine list at the Brewhouse should satisfy any non-beer drinker.

Area Attractions:

• **Lockwood-Mathews Mansion Museum**

   295 West Avenue; Norwalk, CT 06850; 203-838-1434

   America's first chateau, now on the National Historic Register, is a fifty-room Victorian palace with many unusual architectural features.

• **Summer Concert Series**

   Performances are staged at different locations in Norwalk. Call 203-854-7806.

The Bru Room at BAR

254 Crown Street; New Haven, CT 06511; 203-495-8924

Located within a block of Yale University, this pub caters to the casual crowd it attracts from the campus and environs. Decor is industrial: bare concrete walls mixed with exposed brickwork, conduits, and pipes. The menu features brick-oven-baked pizza and one salad.

The Beer: The Bru Room offers BAR Blonde, Pale Ale, AmBAR Ale, Damn Good Stout, and Sweet Potato Ale. Beers are also available in a sampler featuring a five-ounce glass of each variety. If beer isn't your thing, try one of the ten single-malt scotches, including an eighteen-year-old Glenmorangie.

Cottrell Brewing Company

100 Mechanic Street; Pawcatuck, CT 06379; 860-599-8213

Tours: Saturdays at 1 P.M. and 3 P.M.

Owner/brewer Mike LeBaron has worked his magic at Ipswich Brewing Company, Portsmouth Brewery, and Smuttynose. His flagship beer is Old Yankee Ale, an amber style that you can try in Connecticut at the Steak Loft in Mystic, C.C. O'Brien's in Pawcatuck and The Lake in Dayville. As of May 1997, LeBaron's beer will be on tap in Rhode Island.

Essex Brewing Company

34 Industrial Park Road; Niantic, CT 06357; 860-739-2739

Farmington River Brewing Company

102 Filley Street; Bloomfield CT 06002; 860-242-3722

Bill Hodkin admits to being a "recovering attorney," and we talked extensively about exactly how many of our kind are involved in this industry. Bill claims to make one of the best blond ales on the East Coast. Call ahead to see when you can tour his brewery and sample it, as well as his Mahogany ESB and Nut Brown Ale.

The Hammer and Nail Brewers of Connecticut

P.O. Box 877; Watertown, CT 06795-0877; 203-274-5911

Peter Hammer and Kit Nagel (which means "nail" in German) have a clever concept in their company's name and lofty ambitions in their brewery. Located in the century-old Seymour Smith building, Hammer and Nail has produced two brews: Vienna Lager and Brown Ale, which are available in bottles and on tap in Connecticut and Rhode Island.

The Hartford Brewery

35 Pearl Street; Hartford, CT 06103; 860-246-2337

Tours: By appointment

Gift Shop: Open during the pub's regular business hours

Although the atmosphere and decor of the Hartford Brewery are quite casual, the beer selection is anything but relaxed. Owner/brewer Phil Hopkins often has available for your quaffing enjoyment more than twenty types of beer at one time, and he has won the "Best Beer in Hartford" honors for three consecutive years in the readers' poll conducted by the *Hartford Advocate*.

The Beer: The list changes often, but recent creations included Pitbull Golden, Arch Amber, Kolsch, Big Wind Wheat Beer, Bushnell Burton Ale, Sweet Stout, Irish Stout, Imperial Russian Stout, Praying Mantis Porter, Old Nag ESB, and Sinister Sneer. But, you can only get Hopkins' beers at the Brewery.

The Food: Hopkins claims that the recipes here are secret and that chef Norm Sinnock's food is "amazing!" Try these pub-fare appetizers: Cornish pasties (flaky pastry crescents filled with tender beef stew and served with rosemary/red-onion marmalade); "Mussel Brose"

(fresh, native mussels in cream and hard-cider broth); "Pearl Street Ale and Sausage Soup" (bratwurst, potatoes, and three cheeses in a hearty soup made with their ale); and "Roasted Idaho Potato Wedges with Bacchus Barbecue Sauce."

Dinners continue in the traditional vein: Irish stew with whiskey gravy; a roasted half-chicken with the fixings; Devonshire fish-and-oyster pie; peppered roast sirloin of beer with porter au jus.

The Peter Austin brewing system is visible from the bar area at the Hartford Brewery.

Note: Simon says parking on the street is virtually impossible because of the pub's proximity to the Hartford Civic Center, but garages are within walking distance. The atmosphere here is akin to a sports bar, with a bar-sized pool table, pinball machine, and dart boards. The Brewery sponsors a soccer team, two dart teams, and a softball team, and it participates in at least two dozen local charitable events per year.

Area Attractions: Let's hope you like sports, because Hartford hosts a lot of them, all at the Civic Center.

- **Hartford Whalers**
  860-728-3366
  This is a National Hockey League team with pre-season games in September and a regular season from October to April.
- **Connecticut Coyotes**
  860-275-6200
  Professional arena football is played from May to August.
- **Connecticut Sports Museum and Hall of Fame**
  860-724-4918
  Also housed in the civic center (on the second level), this museum's name says it all.

Now let's explore the area's culture and history.

- **The Mark Twain House**
  351 Farmington Avenue; Hartford, CT 06105; 860-493-6411
  This elaborate nineteen-room Victorian mansion features rare interiors by Tiffany and other artists. It's a National Historic Landmark.

- **Old State House**
  800 Main Street; Hartford, CT 06103; 860-522-6766
  The oldest statehouse in the country, this building was designed by Charles Bulfinch. The first written Constitution was produced here.

- **Wadsworth Atheneum**
  600 Main Street; Hartford, CT 01603; 860-278-2670
  The Wadsworth is the oldest public art museum and houses more than 50,000 works.

- **Hartford Stage Company**
  50 Church Street; Hartford, CT 01603; 860-527-5151
  From September to June, see this Tony-Award-winning professional theater company present both new plays and classics.

John Harvard's Brew House

1487 Pleasant Valley Road; Manchester, CT 06040; 860-644-2739

Chef Brad Troxell will offer the same menu as the one featured at the original John Harvard's in Cambridge, Massachusetts, but the daily specials will be different. The beers will be brewed by Rob Leonard, who previously worked at the Cambridge and Framingham locations. His offerings will include All American Light beer, a pale ale, a nut brown, a porter, a stout, and fruit beers in season.

New Haven Brewing Company
The Brewery Restaurant

Elm City Brewing; 458 Grand Avenue; New Haven, CT 06513; 800-ELMCITY

Tours: Saturday at 11 A.M.

Ron Page has been called the Leonardo da Vinci of the New England brewing world because he has been named "New England Homebrewer of the Year" six years in a row. Busy as he is, Page manages to keep more than twelve beers on tap at all times.

The Beer: Past selections have included Connecticut Ale, Golden Ale, Mr. Mike's Light Ale, Elm City Black and Tan, and Blackwell Stout. Obviously the beer is paramount at the Brewery, since I didn't receive the requested menu. But that's okay. If the chef cooks as well as Page brews, the eating has to be good.

Post Road Brewing Company
49 Boston Post Road; Waterford, CT 06385; 860-442-1200

Brad Pierrello brews up Ledge Light, Eagle Alt, Mud Head Brown Ale, Nautilus Porter, Colonel Ledyard Bitter, and seasonals to serve with his menu of daily specials, nachos, chili, steak au poivre, and other pub fare.

Trout Brook Brewing Company and Restaurant
55 Bartholomew Avenue; Hartford, CT 06106; 860-951-1680

Jack Streich, who once worked at Commonwealth Brewing Company, now brews McCarthy's Irish Stout, Thomas Hooker Pale Ale, Mike's Light Ale, Trout Brook ESB, and Trout Brook Cream Ale for this relatively new establishment. The 200-seat restaurant features an enclosed cigar/game room and serves pub fare like wings and nachos, as well as full-fledged entrées like Delmonico steak.

Willimantic Brewing Company and the Main Street Cafe
967 Main Street; Willimantic, CT 06226; 860-423-6777

Cindy and David Wollner are operating this cafe and microbrew bar, offering pub grub, deli sandwiches, burgers, and full dinners of steak, seafood, and sautés. Join them for more than forty American microbrews on draft. "We don't sell any imports," says Cindy, proud of their loyalty to their peers. In summer 1997, the Wollners will begin brewing their own beers, named for the old post office their business inhabits. Selections will include Pony Expresso Stout, Air Mail Ale, and Dog Bite Bitter.

SLATED TO OPEN SOON:

(I'm providing as much information about these establishments as was supplied to me. Call ahead to make sure they're up and running. Where there are no phone numbers, owners ask that hopeful visitors seek the new numbers from directory assistance.)

Indian Neck Brewery

1088 Main Street; Branford, CT 06405

John Harvard's Brew House

540 Riverside Drive; Westport, CT 06880; 203-457-2337

Scheduled for a May 14, 1997, opening.

Nutmeg Brewery

50 Orange Street; New Haven, CT 06510

The second location of the Hartford Brewery is slated for a June 1997 opening. Phil Hopkins will offer different beers than in Hartford but will stay true to his specialty, English ales, turned out on a ten-barrel Easyflow brewing system. Customers will dine on casual New England food in the brick and hardwood ambiance of a converted, turn-of-the-century furniture warehouse with an Art Deco facade. Adult games like darts, foos ball, and billiards are available in the game room. All told, there's a lot to be enjoyed in this 8,000-square-foot "pub."

Olde Wyndham Brewing Company

P.O. Box 14; Windham, CT 06280

Appendixes

Brew-on-Premises Facilities

If you've wondered whether you would enjoy brewing your own beer, but don't want to chance the cost of the equipment to find out, the answer may be a trip to IncrediBREW in Nashua, New Hampshire. Founded in August 1995 by Dave and Nancy Williams, IncrediBREW is the only brew-on-premises facility in New England.

"We have customers who drive from Cape Cod and Springfield, Massachusetts; Bath, Maine; and Hartford, Connecticut," says Dave, who happily stepped off the corporate ladder to open his own company. "IncrediBREW goes beyond the brewpub or brewery tour experience," he claims "because at a brewpub, you get full and have to leave, and at a brewery, the tour is eventually over. Here, you come in and brew for two hours, then come back ten days later to bottle the beer and take it home. We supply all the equipment, recipes [more than sixty-five], do all the prep work, sanitizing, sterilization, and clean-up. You come in and have a good time."

IncrediBREW has played host to organizations, such as the local Porsche Club, that hold their meetings there, then adjourn to brew beer. "Some people enjoy brewing beer at home, but I think that can be too solitary an experience, especially for the novice. About 30 or 40 percent of our customers have brewed at home once or twice, with varying degrees of success. They come to learn more about brewing and to socialize at the same time. There are always other people here to learn from or talk to, and you can sample the beer and make your own."

IncrediBREW
112 Daniel Webster Highway (about 2 miles north of the Pheasant Lane Mall); Nashua, NH 03060; 603-891-2477
Dave and Nancy Williams

BEER-BY-MAIL

If you can't frequent tap houses in your search for good microbrews, and your vacation this year isn't going to allow travel to all the micros or pubs you would like to visit, one option is to join a beer-by-mail club. The following list is one I put together from companies I saw advertised in beer magazines, in newspapers, or on the Internet. I haven't tried any of them and can't, therefore, endorse one over another. Caveat emptor.

- **Ale By Mail** — *800-996-BREW*
  This group provides two six-packs each month. Two-month to twelve-month memberships are available. Benefits include T-shirts, brochures, coasters, and recipes.

- **Brew Tour** — *800-660-TOUR*
  You'll receive two six-packs per month.

- **Beer Across America** — *800-854-BEER*
  This concern bills itself as "The Original Microbrewery Beer of the Month Club." Membership entitles you to a monthly shipment of two six-packs, one from each of two different breweries. A newsletter is included.

- **Brewer's Gourmet** — *800-591-BREW*
  Two six-packs and a newsletter will arrive at your door each month.

- **Foggy Bay Beer Club** — *800-233-0399*
  These folks offer two six-packs per month and *The Fog Horn* newsletter.

- **The Great American Beer Club** — *800-TRY-A-SIP*
  President Doug Doretti chatted with me for a while over the phone and sent me an impressive packet describing his business. You don't have to be locked into a year-long deal right away; instead, you can opt to try GABC for one to five months. There is also a six-month membership that includes a T-shirt, and if you sign up for a twelve-month membership, Doretti will throw in a free month—sort of a brewer's dozen. GABC gives members three four-packs (a dozen twelve-ounce bottles) per month from three different micros, and a newsletter is included.

- **Hogshead Beer Cellars** — *800-992-CLUB*
  Membership means two six-packs per month, along with a newsletter and recipes.
- **Red, White and Brew** — *800-670-BREW*
  You'll receive two six-packs per month, a newsletter, and a complimentary subscription to *Ale Street News.*

THE MODERN BREWER HOME-BREW RECIPES

The Modern Brewer

2304 Massachusetts Avenue; Cambridge, MA 02140; 617-498-0400

This home-brew establishment has been selling supplies to locals for years and is the favorite home-brew supply store of Cambridge Brewing Company's brewer, Will Meyers. Bradd Wheeler, the manager at Modern Brewer graciously let me reprint these recipes.

Modern Brewer Chocolate Raspberry Porter *(Makes five gallons)*

8 pounds English Pale Malt

1 pound Toasted Malt

¾ pound Crystal 90L

½ pound roasted barley

½ pound Chocolate Malt

¾ ounce Northern Brewer hops (60)

½ ounce Willamette hops (30)

6 ounces unsweetened baker's chocolate

½ ounce Goldings hops (15)

Irish Ale Yeast

Prime with 3 cups Chambord raspberry liqueur

Mash grains at 158 degrees Fahrenheit, using 1 quart of water per pound of grain. Sparge with ½ gallon of water per pound of grain and collect 6½ gallons of runnings. Add 1 teaspoon gypsum and 1 teaspoon calcium chloride to the kettle. Add ¾ ounce Northern Brewer hops after the hot break, ½ ounce Willamette hops and 6 ounces unsweetened baker's chocolate for the last thirty minutes, and ½ ounce Goldings hops for the last fifteen minutes. The yeast goes in after the mixture is boiled, cooled, and in the fermenter.

Modern Brewer comments: "This sensual, delicious recipe combines traditional brewing ingredients and some unusual extras like the Chambord and chocolate. Although it can be consumed just a couple of weeks after carbonating, it improves dramatically with aging (one to six months), and still tastes great a year after brewing."

Bradd's Traditional Winter Warmer *(Makes five gallons)*

    11 pounds British Pale Malt
    ½ pound Victory
    ½ pound Toasted
    ½ Crystal 120
    1 ounce Chinook hops (12 percent) 60 min.
    1 ounce Centennial hops (8.7 percent) 30 min.
    1 ounce Centennial hops 5 min.
    1 ounce Cascade Hops (4.1 percent) 5 min.
    Whitbread ale yeast (Wyeast 1098)

Mash grains at 154 degrees Fahrenheit, using 1 quart of water per pound of grain. Sparge with ½ gallon of water per pound of grain and collect 6½ gallons of runnings. Add 1 teaspoon gypsum and 1 teaspoon calcium chloride to the kettle.

Bradd notes that this winter warmer will have an original gravity of 1.065, so the alcohol should be apparent in the nose, along with plenty of spice and citrus notes from the Centennial and Cascade hops.

Modern Brewer Root Beer

    1 ounce Sarsaparilla
    1 ounce sassafras
    1 ounce ginger root

1 ounce birch bark
2 pounds molasses (1 quart)
2 pounds honey (1 quart)
1 pound corn sugar /cane sugar/table sugar

Boil spices and sugars (use any of those mentioned above or a combination up to 1 pound) in 2 gallons of water for thirty minutes to sanitize the root beer, as well as to extract the flavor and aroma from the spices. Cool as you would beer, and add 2 packets of Pasteur Champagne yeast. Bottle immediately and store in a warm place.

After three days, begin checking the carbonation level by sampling a bottle. When the carbonation is at a level you like, chill the root beer to as close to freezing as possible (without actually freezing it). This will stop the fermentation, but *you must store the root beer in a cold place.* Otherwise, fermentation might begin again, and you could end up with exploding bottles. (So if you can't store it cold, drink it fast and keep it away from clean clothes).

What we have described here is the "natural" root beer method. You can also add extract. We vote for the addition of a 4-ounce bottle of root-beer extract. This will give the beverage a taste much closer to that of commercial root beer. Once you have mastered the process, play with the ingredients. The above recipe makes a sweet root beer.

STATE DEPARTMENTS OF TOURISM WEB ADDRESSES

Maine — http://www.state.me.us/decd/tour/
New Hampshire — http://www.VisitNH.gov/
Vermont — http://www.genghis.com/tourism/vermont.htm
Massachusetts — http://www.mass-vacation.com
Connecticut — http://ctguide.atlantic.com/vacguide/
Rhode Island — http://www.visitrhodeisland.com/menu.html

BUSINESS INDEX

RECIPE INDEX

LOCATION INDEX

W